Great Reads for Book Clubs: Recommended Books for Reading Groups

KATHRYN COPE

Copyright © 2016 Kathryn Cope

All rights reserved.

ISBN-13: 978-1520169484

CONTENTS

Introduction	1
Categories	3
1984	7
All the Light We Cannot See	12
Americanah	17
And the Mountains Echoed	21
The Art of Racing in the Rain	26
The Buried Giant	30
The Catcher in the Rye	36
Everything I Never Told You	41
The Fault in our Stars	46
The Girl on the Train	51
The Girls	56
The Glorious Heresies	61
The Goldfinch	67
Gone Girl	72
The Great Gatsby	76
The Guernsey Literary & Potato Peel Pie Society	80
The Heart Goes Last	85

The Help	90
The Humans	95
The Husband's Secret	100
I Know Why the Caged Bird Sings	104
The Invention of Wings	110
Life After Life	114
The Light Between Oceans	119
The Loney	123
A Man Called Ove	127
The Miniaturist	131
My Brilliant Friend	136
My Name is Lucy Barton	141
The Paying Guests	146
A Place Called Winter	150
Room	155
The Shock of the Fall	159
The Snow Child	163
Station Eleven	167
The Storied Life of A.J. Fikry	171
The Sympathizer	175
The Tiger's Wife	181

The Turn of the Screw	186
The Underground Railroad	191
We Are All Completely Beside Ourselves	197
We Were Liars	202
The Woman in Black	207
The Year of the Runaways	211
Bibliography	216
About the Author	224

INTRODUCTION

There are few things more rewarding than getting together with a group of like-minded people and discussing a good book. Book club meetings, at their best, are vibrant, passionate affairs. Each member will bring along a different perspective and ideally there will be heated debate. A surprising number of book club members, however, report that their meetings have been a disappointment. Either their choice has failed to live up to the publisher's hype, or group members enjoyed the book but could think of astonishingly little to say about it. As most book clubs only meet once a month, a wasted choice is frustrating for everyone.

The aim of this companion guide is to take the hard work out of your book club meetings by suggesting titles that should spark fruitful discussion. Making this selection has involved a careful balancing act between literary quality and book club suitability. Through my own experiences of book clubs I have learned that great books do not always make great book club choices. After choosing some personal favourites to share with my group in my early book group days I quickly realised that, while these novels were undoubtedly beautifully written, they did not provoke scintillating debate. Meanwhile other titles which were hailed as ideal for book groups by their savvy publishing houses may have touched on interesting subject matter but proved a let-down when it came to the quality of the writing. Each title in this guide has been chosen for its literary quality but also for what it has to offer in the way of discussion. I cannot promise that every member of your book club will enjoy every choice. What I can guarantee is that each title has literary merit and will spark plenty of discussion.

The entries in this guide are listed alphabetically according to title. The chosen books deliberately cover a variety of historical periods, countries and subjects, and include a broad range of writing styles. While the majority of the titles were published in the last few years, a sprinkling of classics has been thrown in for good measure. They span humour, tragedy, the uplifting and the controversial – sometimes all within the same novel. Some of the titles are very accessible and others are more challenging. Only novels that are extremely experimental in style have been avoided. Difference of opinion in a group is a good thing but not when members dislike the style of a book so much that they feel it is impossible to plough through it.

The layout of this guide is designed to make choosing your next read as easy as possible. Each entry includes an approximate page count, to give your group a general idea of how long it will take to read. There is also an 'in a nutshell' description which sums up the mood and subject of the book in a few words, as well as a more detailed blurb and a list of the novel's themes. Perhaps most crucially, 15 thought-provoking discussion questions are included for every entry to make sure that your group doesn't run short of interesting discussion angles. While the book descriptions don't include significant spoilers, the discussion questions inevitably do. For this reason, don't be tempted to read the discussion questions before you have read the novel. Further reading recommendations are also included based on the novel's subject matter or style. Finally, a 'compare and contrast to' section suggests other titles in the guide that this book could be productively compared to, allowing your group to draw parallels between the books that they have read.

To make your choice even easier, a list of categories is provided on the next page. This enables your group to choose a title according to genre, page length, or even based upon the time of year you will be reading it. Happy reading and debating!

Kathryn Cope, 2016

Categories

Quick Reads (250 pages or less)

The Catcher in the Rye; The Great Gatsby; The Guernsey Literary and Potato Peel Pie Society; My Name is Lucy Barton; The Turn of the Screw; We Were Liars; The Woman in Black

Hefty Tomes (500 pages or more but worth it)

All the Light We Cannot See; The Goldfinch; Life After Life

Historical Novels (pre-1970s)

All the Light We Cannot See; And the Mountains Echoed; The Buried Giant; The Girls; The Guernsey Literary and Potato Peel Pie Society; The Help; The Invention of Wings; Life After Life; The Light Between Oceans; The Miniaturist; My Brilliant Friend; The Paying Guests; A Place Called Winter; The Snow Child; The Underground Railroad; The Woman in Black

War and its Aftermath

All the Light We Cannot See; And the Mountains Echoed; The Buried Giant; The Guernsey Literary and Potato Peel Pie Society; Life After Life; The Light Between Oceans; The Paying Guests; The Sympathizer; The Tiger's Wife

Racial/cultural identity

Americanah; Everything I Never Told You; The Help; I Know Why the Caged Bird Sings; The Invention of Wings; The Sympathizer; The Tiger's Wife; The Underground Railroad; The Year of the Runaways

Coming-of-Age

All the Light We Cannot See; The Catcher in the Rye; Everything I Never

Told You; The Fault in Our Stars; The Girls; The Glorious Heresies; The Goldfinch; I Know Why the Caged Bird Sings; The Invention of Wings; My Brilliant Friend; The Loney; The Shock of the Fall; We Were Liars

Family Dynamics

Everything I Never Told You; The Girls; The Humans; The Husband's Secret; My Name is Lucy Barton; Room; The Shock of the Fall; The Storied Life of A.J. Fikry; We Were Liars

Friendship

The Guernsey Literary and Potato Peel Pie Society; The Help; The Invention of Wings; A Man Called Ove; My Brilliant Friend; The Snow Child

Love Stories

1984; Americanah; The Fault in Our Stars; The Glorious Heresies; The Goldfinch; The Great Gatsby; The Guernsey Literary and Potato Peel Pie Society; The Humans; The Light Between Oceans; The Paying Guests; A Place Called Winter; The Storied Life of A.J. Fikry; We Were Liars

Crime

The Girl on the Train; The Girls; The Glorious Heresies; The Goldfinch; Gone Girl; The Paying Guests; Room

Classics

1984; The Catcher in the Rye; The Great Gatsby; I Know Why the Caged Bird Sings; The Turn of the Screw

Gothic/Supernatural

The Loney; The Turn of the Screw; The Woman in Black

Fantasy/Dystopian Fiction

1984; The Buried Giant; The Heart Goes Last; Station Eleven

Tearjerkers

All the Light We Cannot See; And the Mountains Echoed; The Art of Racing in the Rain; The Fault in Our Stars; The Guernsey Literary and Potato Peel Pie Society; The Humans; The Light Between Oceans; A Man Called Ove; The Shock of the Fall; The Snow Child; The Storied Life of A.J. Fikry; We Are All Completely Beside Ourselves

Humorous (although be warned, several of these also come under tearjerkers)

The Art of Racing in the Rain; The Catcher in the Rye; The Fault in Our Stars; The Glorious Heresies; The Guernsey Literary and Potato Peel Pie Society; The Heart Goes Last; The Help; The Humans; A Man Called Ove; The Shock of the Fall; The Storied Life of A.J. Fikry

Gritty Realism

The Glorious Heresies; My Brilliant Friend; The Girls; The Year of the Runaways

Realist/Fantasy Combos

All the Light We Cannot See; The Humans; Life After Life; The Miniaturist; The Snow Child; The Tiger's Wife; The Underground Railroad

Quirky Narrators

The Art of Racing in the Rain; The Catcher in the Rye; The Humans; Room; The Shock of the Fall; We Are All Completely Beside Ourselves; We Were Liars

Fiendish Plot Twists

The Girl on the Train; Gone Girl; The Husband's Secret; We Are All Completely Beside Ourselves; We Were Liars

Summer Reads

The Catcher in the Rye; The Girl on the Train; The Girls; The Great Gatsby; My Brilliant Friend; The Paying Guests; We Were Liars

Wintry Reads

The Buried Giant; The Goldfinch; Life After Life; The Loney; A Place Called Winter; The Snow Child; The Woman in Black

1984
by George Orwell

FIRST PUBLISHED

1949

LENGTH

400 pages

SETTING

1984 - London, England (renamed Airstrip One)

ABOUT THE BOOK

The year is 1984. Winston Smith, Orwell's unlikely hero, lives in Airstrip One (formerly London) in the state of Oceania. Led by a mysterious figurehead known as Big Brother, Oceania is constantly at war with one of the two other world states: Eastasia and Eurasia. Under the totalitarian regime of Big Brother and the Party, privacy and individual freedom are strictly forbidden. Telescreens continually monitor the behaviour of citizens while even freedom of thought is restricted through the introduction of a new language, Newspeak. In his job at the Ministry of Truth, Winston helps to perpetuate the Party's propaganda by falsifying documents in order to 'change history'.

Winston's rebellion against this grim and oppressive life begins when he starts to keep a diary of his thoughts. He then embarks on a strictly forbidden love affair with Julia, a young woman who also secretly hates the Party and all that it stands for. As their affair intensifies, Winston becomes increasingly determined to join the Brotherhood, an underground group of rebels who plan to overthrow the Party. His plan, however, will lead to certain arrest and unthinkable punishments if he is caught.

1984 is a fictional warning of the dangers of totalitarian governments, inspired by Orwell's first-hand observations of oppressive communist regimes in Spain and Russia. Over 60 years after its original publication the novel remains astonishingly ahead of its time. Orwell's critique of the human tendency to abuse political power remains depressingly relevant, while his presentation of a world in which citizens are constantly monitored is often referenced in current debates about CCTV usage and internet privacy. It is a testament to this novel's enduring power that some of its made-up vocabulary has become an accepted part of the English language. Even those who have never heard of George Orwell will have seen the reality TV programme 'Big Brother' which, while just about as far from Orwell's original novel in tone as is possible, still captures the nightmarish concept of life under continual surveillance. Orwell's classic was also the inspiration and benchmark for all the dystopian novels and films that followed in its wake. The recent flurry of popular dystopian trilogies (*The Hunger Games*, *Divergent*, *The Maze Runner* etc.) and even 'The Lego Movie' are all part of the legacy of *1984*. While Orwell's bleak warning of what the future may hold is far from an uplifting read, it is an absolute must for literature lovers as well as those interested in debates about personal freedom.

ABOUT THE AUTHOR

George Orwell was the pen name of the British writer Eric Arthur Blair. He was born in 1903 in India, where his father worked as a civil servant, but his family moved to England in 1907. After attending Eton, Orwell served with the Indian Imperial police in Burma from 1922 to 1927. He then moved to Paris for two years before returning to England. While working on a number of literary projects, Orwell took a range of jobs from private tutor and schoolteacher to bookshop assistant. In 1936 he travelled to Spain to fight for the Republicans, where he was wounded. His health never fully recovered. During the Second World War Orwell served in the home guard and worked for the BBC Eastern service. In 1943 he became literary editor of the *London Tribune* and he also wrote for the *Observer* and the *Manchester Evening News*. He died of tuberculosis at the age of forty-six.

During his relatively short life Orwell produced an impressive canon of literary work. While he is best remembered for the classic novels *Animal Farm* and *1984*, a great deal of his work was non-fiction, including journalism, essays and full-length books. All of his work was informed by his left-wing and anti-totalitarian political beliefs.

IN A NUTSHELL

A bleak but astonishingly perceptive vision of the future

THEMES

The abuse of power; class inequality; xenophobia; the importance of history and memory; the role of technology in oppression; personal freedom & the right to privacy; the role of language in shaping thought

DISCUSSION QUESTIONS

1/ The story is told from Winston's point of view but through a third person narrator. Why does Orwell use this form of narration? What is the overall tone and what impact does this have on the reader?

2/ What characteristics make Winston an unusual male protagonist? Why is he a suitable choice for Orwell's story? Do you consider him to be a hero?

3/ Winston's decision to keep a secret diary marks the beginning of his revolt against Big Brother. Discuss the role of words and literature in the Party's regime of oppression. Why is writing in a journal such a revolutionary act?

4/ What role does continuous war (or the appearance of it) play in the Party's regime?

5/ Discuss the impact the Party's regulations have on personal relationships (love, sex, friendship and family).

6/ Discuss the significance of the nursery rhyme that Winston struggles to remember and the coral paperweight.

7/ In the early stages of the novel Winston fantasises about raping and murdering Julia. What other violent and misogynistic thoughts does he express? Why do you think Orwell includes these passages? Does Winston's attitude to women change as the story progresses?

8/ What did you think of Orwell's portrayal of Julia? How do you think the author wanted the reader to view her?

9/ Discuss Winston's feelings for Julia and the way she transforms his life. Would it have been better for him if he had never met her? Does his eventual betrayal of Julia mean he didn't genuinely love her? Could any love withstand such circumstances?

10/ Winston progresses from perceiving the proles as less than human to believing that they are the only hope for the future. Do you think his faith in the proles is justified? Did you see anything problematic in Orwell's portrayal of the working classes?

11/ How did you feel about the ending of the novel? Did you expect Winston's rebellion against the Party to succeed?

12/ George Orwell unapologetically used his fiction to express his political convictions. What is he specifically critiquing in the novel? How politically persuasive is *1984*? Did you find it overtly polemical at any point?

13/ Was there anything you didn't like about Orwell's writing style in *1984*? While the novel is undoubtedly visionary, is it in any way dated?

14/ In Orwell's dark vision of the future, which aspects struck you as the most perceptive? What is most frightening? How close or far away is our current society to Orwell's vision of 1984? Is there a chance that society may become more like *1984* as time goes on?
15/ What would lurk in your own version of Room 101?

FURTHER READING

Fahrenheit 451, Ray Bradbury
Do Androids Dream of Electric Sheep?, Philip K. Dick
Brave New World, Aldous Huxley
The Handmaid's Tale, Margaret Atwood
Never Let Me Go, Kazuo Ishiguro

COMPARE & CONTRAST TO

The Heart Goes Last for its vision of the future – particularly the roles of technology, freewill and sex

All the Light We Cannot See
by Anthony Doerr

FIRST PUBLISHED

2015

LENGTH

544 pages

SETTING

France and Germany pre- and post-World War II

ABOUT THE BOOK

This Pulitzer Prize-winning novel tells the story of two characters: Marie-Laure LeBlanc and Werner Pfennig. Marie-Laure is a blind girl who is brought up in France by her locksmith father while Werner grows up in an orphanage in Germany. When World War II breaks out, Marie-Laure becomes involved in aiding the French Resistance while Werner tries to better himself by becoming a communications technician in the German army. Their stories converge when Werner is sent to Saint-Malo to track illegal radio transmissions.

Through his two protagonists the author portrays the experience of the Second World War from both a French and German perspective. While Marie-Laure's story highlights the bravery of those who took part in the French Resistance, Werner's tale illustrates the pressures put upon German citizens to conform to Nazi ideology. Although a novel about war, *All the Light We Cannot See*, at times, has the feel of a fairytale or fable. This is partly due to the beauty of Doerr's language and partly down to a subplot concerning the 'Sea of Flames': a huge diamond which is rumoured to be both blessed and cursed. Moving and charming, this is war fiction which will appeal to those who would normally avoid the genre.

ABOUT THE AUTHOR

Anthony Doerr is an American author who grew up in Ohio, and now lives in Boise, Idaho, with his wife and two sons. His other work includes the short story collections *Memory Wall* and *The Shell Collector*, a memoir (*Four Seasons in Rome*) and the novel *About Grace*. In 2007 Doerr was named by Granta as one of 21 best young American novelists. *All the Light We Cannot See* won the Pulitzer Prize for fiction in 2015 and the Andrew Carnegie Medal for Excellence in Fiction.

IN A NUTSHELL

History meets parable in this beautifully written coming-of-age tale

THEMES

As well as the brutality of war, Doerr explores the universal themes of moral courage, love, loss, the beauty of the natural world and the endurance of the human spirit. Recurring imagery used throughout the novel (light and darkness, birds, spirals and mollusks - to name but a few) beautifully underlines these themes.

DISCUSSION QUESTIONS

1/ On one level, 'All the Light We Cannot See' refers to the topic of the radio science broadcast Werner hears as a child. In what other ways does the novel examine the idea of light which exists but cannot be seen by the naked eye?

2/ Through his vividly sensory style, the author seems to suggest that Marie-Laure's perception of the world is more profound as a result of her lack of sight. Did you find this depiction of how it feels to be blind convincing or somewhat romanticised?

3/ Marie-Laure and Werner experience very different childhoods.

In what way does their upbringing influence the young adults they become? How much choice does Werner ultimately have over the path his life takes?

4/ Doerr states that, although he deliberately created Werner as a morally flawed character, he hoped that the reader would be rooting for him throughout the novel. Why do you think the author wanted this? Did you still have sympathy for Werner, despite his poor moral choices?

5/ In what way do Frederick and Jutta act as Werner's slumbering conscience in the novel? At what point does Werner's conscience awaken?

6/ *All the Light We Cannot See* is constructed of extremely short chapters which move back and forth in viewpoint and timeframe. Did you like the structure of the novel or find it disorienting? Did the brevity of the chapters make it more readable? Why do you think Doerr chose to include the voices of more minor characters, such as Etienne, von Rumpel, Frau Elena and Volkheimer? Did the extra viewpoints add breadth to the novel, or would you have preferred the author to stick with the alternating perspectives of Marie-Laure and Werner?

7/ The novel celebrates the power of radio, recreating a time when the transmission of music and human voices still seemed miraculous. What role does radio play in the novel's plot? What motivates Marie-Laure to start reading into the radio receiver when she is trapped in the attic? Did the novel renew your appreciation of radio as a medium of entertainment?

8/ The novel suggests that there is a link between an appreciation for the natural world and moral purity. Discuss this connection in relation to the characters of Marie-Laure, Frederick and Etienne. How is their sense of wonder at the beauty of nature expressed? How does their appreciation of natural beauty differ from von Rumpel's? Try to find a passage where the author's love of nature shines through in the text.

9/ Bravery and sacrifice are recurring themes in the novel. Discuss the various sacrifices that the characters make – whether for country, or for loved ones. Who did you feel made the greatest sacrifice in the novel?

10/ Why do you think the author chose to include the subplot involving the Sea of Flames? What does this storyline add to the novel? Do you think the curse on the diamond is genuine? Why does Marie-Laure give Werner the key for the grotto after she leaves the Sea of Flames there?

11/ Although the plot of the novel focuses mainly on the German Occupation of France and the horrors of warfare, Doerr slips subtle references to the fate of the Jewish people into his text. Discuss the points in the novel where he does this. Are these references to the Holocaust inadequate, or all the more powerful for their subtlety?

12/ After the war Jutta and Frederick's mother both feel guilt and shame about who they are. Why do they feel this conflict over their identity and is their sense of guilt justified?

13/ Werner dreams of using his scientific talents to benefit the world but ends up employing his gift in a far less noble way. Discuss the way scientific knowledge serves both good and evil purposes in the novel. Is there an overriding message about the moral responsibilities involved in developing science and technology?

14/ Discuss the way in which the technological nature of Werner's military role detaches him from the horrific reality of combat. Does his situation have parallels with contemporary warfare?

15/ Were you surprised by the author's decision to end the novel in the near-present? Did this add to the reading experience or would you have preferred the story to end in the 1940s? Was the novel's overall tone ultimately sombre or uplifting?

FURTHER READING

Charlotte Gray, Sebastian Faulks

The Nightingale, Kristin Hannah
Citadel, Kate Mosse
A Thread of Grace, Mary Doria Russell
Resistance, Anita Shreve

COMPARE & CONTRAST TO

The Guernsey Literary and Potato Peel Pie Society – for its portrayal of the resistance of ordinary people during World War II or *The Tiger's Wife* for the combination of fable and realism

Americanah
by Chimamanda Ngozi Adichie

FIRST PUBLISHED

2013

LENGTH

400 pages

SETTING

Nigeria and the USA

ABOUT THE BOOK

Ifemulu and Obinze are teenagers when they meet and fall in love in the Nigerian city of Lagos. They both go on to University in Nigeria but, increasingly frustrated by teaching strikes, Ifemelu applies for a scholarship to continue her studies at Princeton in the USA. Obinze, who worships all things American, encourages his girlfriend, planning to join her when he has graduated. When the time comes, however, he finds he is unable to secure an American visa.Spanning thirteen years, *Americanah* follows the individual paths of Ifemelu and Obinze as they make lives for themselves without each other. Nevertheless, neither of them is able to forget their first love.

Shortlisted for the Baileys Women's Prize for Fiction, *Americanah* is a powerful love story exploring identity, race and the quest to find a place to call home. While satirising the racial attitudes of the USA from a Nigerian perspective, Adichie also doesn't flinch from exposing the corrupt nature of Nigerian society where it is impossible to get on through merit alone. One of the great strengths of *Americanah* is that it highlights a whole range of attitudes towards race – from out-and-out racism to liberal guilt and over-zealously applied positive discrimination. For book groups, the novel raises many thought-provoking questions about our attitudes to people of other races.

ABOUT THE AUTHOR

Adichie was born to Igbo parents in Nigeria in 1977. After studying medicine and pharmacy at the University of Nigeria for eighteen months, she moved to the U.S. to study communication and political science. She graduated from Eastern Connecticut State University in 2001 and went on to complete a master's degree in creative writing at John Hopkins University, Baltimore. Her first novel, *Purple Hibiscus* (2003), was longlisted for the Booker Prize. In 2007 this was followed by *Half of a Yellow Sun* which won the Orange Prize for Fiction. In 2010 Adichie was named in the *New Yorker* as one of the best 20 writers under the age of forty.

THEMES

The immigrant experience; racial & cultural identity; the many permeations of racism; interracial relationships; love; American culture; nepotism and corruption

DISCUSSION QUESTIONS

1/ Ifemelu is impulsive, headstrong and flawed. Could you sympathise with her as a character? Did you always understand her motivations?

2/ How does Obinze's personality and background contrast with Ifemelu's? What attracts him to her?

3/ In what way does Adichie critique Nigerian society in the novel? If you are familiar with Nigeria, did you feel this was an accurate picture? If not, did you learn anything new about Nigeria from reading *Americanah*?

4/ Much of Ifemelu's story is told through flashbacks while she is having her hair braided at a salon. Why do you think the author chose this non-chronological structure for her story? Did you find it effective?

5/ What does Ifemelu imagine life in the USA will be like? From what sources has she accumulated her preconceptions? In what ways does the USA fail to meet her expectations?

6/ Discuss the difficulties Ifemelu and Obinze experience in the USA and the UK respectively. What are the similarities and differences between their experiences? How do these experiences impact upon their later life choices?

7/ In the USA Ifemelu embarks on romantic relationships with Curt, a white American, and Blaine, an American African. What initially attracts her to them and why don't these relationships work out? What is it that ultimately makes Ifemelu and Obinze so compatible?

8/ Although Aunty Uju is an intelligent and capable woman she twice becomes dependent upon men who are unworthy of her: the Nigerian General and then Bartholomew. What do these choices of relationship say about the opportunities open to her, first in Nigeria and then in the USA?

9/ Adichie seems to suggest that many Nigerians who emigrate to new countries lose their sense of identity. Discuss this idea in relation to the characters of Aunty Uju, Bartholomew, Emenike and Ginika.

10/ Discuss the way in which Ifemelu initially feels pressured to Americanise herself in the USA. At what point does she decide to stop doing this and how does this decision express itself? Why does Adichie begin her novel with Ifemelu's visit to the hair salon?

11/ Adichie uses Ifemelu's blog as a device for highlighting the politics surrounding racial identity. Did this device work for you? Did the novel as a whole make you think more deeply about the nuances of race?

12/ Ifemelu humorously observes the way many Americans try to be politically correct by avoiding referring to race at all. Discuss the examples she gives of this phenomenon. Do you agree that liberal white Americans and Europeans tend to overdo positive discrimination by pretending that they don't notice race or skin colour? Is there a happy medium between this attitude and racism? What do you feel are acceptable terms to use to describe another person's race or cultural identity?

13/ Obinze decides to return to Lagos and builds an enviable life there. How does he feel about his success?

14/ What does the term 'Americanah' mean in Nigeria? Does Ifemelu inevitably become an Americanah herself? When she returns to Nigeria, how have her perceptions of her home country changed?

15/ At the end of the novel Obinze turns his life upside down to be with Ifemelu. Did you think that their reunion provided a fitting end to the novel? How did you feel about Obinze walking away from his family?

FURTHER READING

Half of a Yellow Sun, Chimamanda Ngozi Adichie
The Memory of Love, Aminatta Forna
Taduno's Song, Odafe Atogun
Homegoing, Yaa Gyasi
Dust, Yvonne Adhiambo Owuor

COMPARE & CONTRAST TO

The Year of the Runaways for its depiction of the immigrant experience or *The Sympathizer* for the novel's critique of American culture

And the Mountains Echoed
by Khaled Hosseini

FIRST PUBLISHED

2013

LENGTH

416 pages

SETTING

Afghanistan, Paris, Greece and California from 1949 to the present day

ABOUT THE BOOK

This sweeping and ambitious novel, which interweaves many narratives, fittingly begins with an act of storytelling. It is 1952 and Saboor, who lives in the Afghan village of Shadbagh, tells his two children a fable about a man who gives up his favourite child to an ogre. The story's purpose is to prepare the children for what is soon to befall them. In order to survive the harsh winter ahead, Saboor has agreed to sell his three-year-old daughter, Pari, to a rich couple in Kabul.

The rest of the story centres around Saboor's momentous decision and the impact it has on those involved. Abdullah, Pari's older brother, is bereft without his beloved sister. Nabi, Abdullah's uncle, finds himself shunned by his family and has to confront his ulterior motives for proposing the adoption in the first place. Nila, Pari's new mother, discovers that the acquisition of a child does not satisfy her restless spirit. Meanwhile Pari, unaware of the existence of her birth family, struggles with the inexplicable feeling that something crucial is missing from her life.

Woven into this central plot are a number of subplots which all turn out to be linked in some way to the story of Pari and Abdullah. These include the stories of Parwana, Saboor's second wife, who harbours a devastating secret; Markos Varvaris, a Greek plastic surgeon, who travels the world operating on children with facial disfigurements; a pair of Afghan-American cousins who return to Afghanistan to reclaim their inheritance; and Adel, the lonely son of an Afghan warlord. *And the Mountains Echoed* is, however, much more than a series of loosely linked short stories. Hosseini takes these apparently disparate strands, ranging across the globe and the decades, and weaves them together into a beautiful and complex tapestry. Each narrative expands upon the last, enriching the novel's exploration of love, loss, exile and sacrifice. Most interestingly of all, in a novel that revolves around moral dilemmas of one sort or another, the author refuses to offer moral certainties. Hosseini presents the reader with a cast of compelling yet flawed characters who do not always act in the way that might be expected. Even the most likeable characters are capable of selfishness and sometimes fail to do the right thing while out-and-out 'villains' are shown performing good works, although not always for the right reasons. In the process, the author raises many thorny questions about what constitutes a 'good' person.

Fans of Hosseini's previous novels, *The Kite Runner* and *A Thousand Splendid Suns*, will not be disappointed by *And the Mountains Echoed*. Once again, the author vividly brings alive the country of his birth within the framework of a compelling and moving story. In this third novel, however, the Afghan-American author has upped his game, achieving an emotional complexity that echoes in the reader's mind long after finishing the last page.

ABOUT THE AUTHOR

Khaled Hosseini was born in Kabul, Afghanistan in 1965. As his father was a diplomat with the Afghan foreign ministry, the Hosseini family moved around during his childhood – to Tehran, then back to Kabul and in 1976, to Paris. As the Hosseini's were on the brink of returning to Kabul in 1980, Afghanistan underwent a bloody communist coup and was invaded by the Soviet army. The Hosseini family were granted political asylum in the United States and moved to San Jose, California. In the process they lost all of their property in Afghanistan and were forced to live on welfare for a short period.

Although Hosseini loved literature, after graduating he took a bachelor's degree in biology and went on to complete a medical degree. He began practising medicine in 1996. In 2003, his first novel, *The Kite Runner* was published. It became an international bestseller and was adapted into a film in 2007. His follow-up novel, *A Thousand Splendid Suns* was published in 2007 and also became a huge bestseller. Hosseini became a Goodwill Envoy for the United Nations Refugee Agency in 2006 and has also established the Khaled Hosseini Foundation, a charity which provides humanitarian assistance to the people of Afghanistan.

IN A NUTSHELL

A morally complex tale of Afghan life

THEMES

Love and the various forms it may take; parent/child & sibling relationships; loss; sacrifice; exile; charity; moral responsibility; war and its aftermath; beauty

DISCUSSION QUESTIONS

1/ The novel opens with Saboor telling his children a story. How does this fable reflect the course of action he is about to take and his feelings about it? What do Saboor's storytelling abilities tell us about his deeper nature?

2/ How did you feel about Saboor's decision to give Pari up to the Wahdatis? Is his assumption that they can offer her a better life misplaced? Would Pari have been better off remaining with her birth family?

3/ Abdullah and Pari are both haunted by a sense of loss after their separation. Discuss the different ways this affects them and the impact it has on their future lives.

4/ Although the separation of Abdullah and Pari lies at the heart of the story, the novel intertwines many other characters and storylines. Which character and storyline was your favourite and why?

5/ The novel's narrative moves back and forth in time and across continents. Did this shifting in time and location unite the novel or fragment it? What are the common threads and how do they inform each other?

6/ On first meeting Nila Wahdati, Abdullah detects that there is "something deeply splintered" beneath her glamorous surface. How did you feel about Nila and her actions? Does she have any redeeming features?

7/ While Nabi dreams of a future with Nila Wahdati, he ends up devoting his life to Seleiman. Discuss the way the relationship between the two men develops over the years. What is the author suggesting about love and the different forms it can take?

8/ Several of the characters experience a conflict between duty and freedom. Discuss the sacrifices Parwana, Nabi, Pari Jr., Markos and Thalia make in order to care for others. Are their motives entirely selfless?

9/ Contrasting with the theme of self-sacrifice in the novel are recurring images of abandonment. Which characters abandon others in the novel and why? Do they suffer for their actions?

10/ Discuss the way in which well-intentioned characters in the novel sometimes fail to do the right thing while less admirable characters perform good deeds, although not necessarily for the right reasons. How does this relate to the novel's epigraph by Rumi: "Out beyond ideas/ of wrongdoing and rightdoing, / there is a field. / I'll meet you there."?

11/ Markos observes that, "Beauty is an enormous, unmerited gift given randomly, stupidly." How is this point illustrated in the novel?

12/ The character of Idris bears a number of similarities to the author of the novel, who also left Afghanistan as a child, studied medicine and now lives in the USA. Do you think Idris's feelings about what he witnesses in Afghanistan reflect Hosseini's own sense of survivor's guilt?

13/ When he visits Afghanistan, Idris is moved by Roshi's plight and vows to help her. Once he returns to the USA, however, his experience in Kabul loses its power and his determination to help Roshi fades. Did his failure to make good on his promise surprise you? Did you reassess his character in the light of this change of heart? What do you think the author is saying about humanitarianism in general?

14/ The novel comes full circle when Abdullah and Pari are reunited as adults. What impact does Abdullah's dementia have on this 'happy ending'? Did you find the conclusion satisfying?

15/ What did you find most striking about Hosseini's portrayal of Afghanistan? How does the author convey the country's war-torn history without setting the main action within wartime? Did reading this novel expand your understanding of Afghanistan and its people?

FURTHER READING

The Kite Runner, Khaled Hosseini
A Thousand Splendid Suns, Khaled Hosseini
Born under a Million Shadows, Andrea Busfield
The Little Coffee Shop of Kabul, Deborah Rodriguez
What Changes Everything, Masha Hamilton

COMPARE & CONTRAST TO

The Husband's Secret for its exploration of complex moral dilemmas and their outcomes

The Art of Racing in the Rain
by Garth Stein

FIRST PUBLISHED

2008

LENGTH

320 pages

SETTING

Seattle, USA

ABOUT THE BOOK

At the beginning of *The Art of Racing in the Rain* its narrator, Enzo (who happens to be a dog), reveals that he is ready to cast off the shackles of his canine life and be reincarnated as a man. In flashback he then relates the details of the life he has spent with his beloved master, Denny. Denny is a racing car driver and Enzo shares his master's passion for the sport. Enzo describes how their bachelor routines are disrupted when Denny falls in love with Eve and they have a daughter, Zoe. Just as Enzo begins to see the merits in his new domestic arrangements, however, life deals Denny a series of devastating blows. Trapped in his voiceless canine body, Enzo is powerless to do anything but observe and offer his unwavering love and support to his master.

Enzo's canine perspective works on many levels. While allowing some humorous observations on the peculiarities of human behaviour, his narrative also offers the kind of insight into the human condition that we humans are generally too busy rushing around to consider. Using his master's fearless approach to racing as an analogy, Enzo offers many wise musings on life and the best way to live it. Given this insight into the narrator's interior life, readers cannot fail to be struck by the irony in his ultimate wish to be reincarnated as a man. While Enzo despises himself for his canine characteristics, the reader sees much to admire and emulate in his capacity for love, loyalty and compassion.

An unashamed tearjerker, *The Art of Racing in the Rain* has been translated into over 30 languages and spent more than three years on the *New York Times* bestseller list. Such was the novel's success that it was also adapted into a YA version (*Racing in the Rain*) and an illustrated version for young children (*Enzo Races in the Rain!*). Dog lovers (and indeed anyone with a heart) should prepare to sob uncontrollably over its final pages.

ABOUT THE AUTHOR

Garth Stein was born in Los Angeles and raised in Seattle. Before becoming a full-time writer, he was a documentary filmmaker. He is also one of the founders of Seattle7Writers, a charity dedicated to encouraging literacy and writing. Stein's other novels include *Raven Stole the Moon*, *How Evan Broke his Head and Other Secrets* and *A Sudden Light*. He lives in Seattle with his wife, three sons and their dog.

IN A NUTSHELL

A heart-wrenching celebration of life and the bond between humans and their canine companions

THEMES

Love; loss; mortality; the endurance of the human (and canine) spirit

DISCUSSION QUESTIONS

1/ Enzo reveals a number of narrative spoilers at the beginning of his story. What are they and how does this affect the reader's experience of the novel?

2/ Enzo sometimes despises himself for being a dog and underappreciates his finer qualities. What superior qualities does

Enzo possess? What lessons could many humans learn from him?

3/ Is Enzo a reliable narrator? In what way is his narrative coloured by his loyalties?

4/ How would the novel differ if it were told from Denny's point of view? Would it be as compelling? Are there any disadvantages of telling a story from a dog's perspective?

5/ What is 'the art of racing in the rain'? How does the novel's title relate to Enzo's approach to life?

6/ How does Eve transform the lives of Denny and Enzo? Discuss Enzo's changing attitude towards her.

7/ What does Zoe's stuffed zebra come to represent for Enzo?

8/ One of Enzo's favourite mantras is, "That which you manifest is before you." What does he mean by this and do you agree with this philosophy?

9/ Do you think Denny was in any way responsible for what happened with Annika? Did you have any sympathy for Annika's character?

10/ Discuss the way Maxwell and Trish treat Denny after Eve's death. Is their response in any way understandable? What are their reasons for instigating a custody battle with Denny?

11/ Denny is placed in an impossible position when he has to choose between pursuing custody of Zoe or facing possible imprisonment. How did you feel about the course of action he takes? What would you have done in his position?

12/ By the end of the novel Enzo no longer believes that a race car driver has to be selfish in order to be successful. What brings him to this realisation?

13/ Enzo believes that we die when we have accomplished everything that we need to in a particular life. What do you think of this concept?

14/ How did you feel about Enzo's death? Could you empathise with his desire to be free from the limitations of life as a dog? Do you think life as a human will meet his expectations?

15/ Is this novel a sentimentalised portrait of the relationship between dogs and their owners, or did you find it emotionally truthful?

FURTHER READING

Lily and the Octopus, Steven Rowley
A Dog's Purpose, W. Bruce Cameron
Spill Simmer Falter Wither, Sara Baume
Jonathan Unleashed by Meg Rosoff
How to Look for a Lost Dog, Ann M. Martin

COMPARE & CONTRAST TO

The Humans for its outsider's perspective on human life

The Buried Giant
by Kazuo Ishiguro

FIRST PUBLISHED

2015

LENGTH

353 pages

SETTING

The Dark Ages, Britain

ABOUT THE BOOK

The Dark Ages conjured up in *The Buried Giant* is a strange and slightly sinister world. Although Britons and Saxons live peacefully alongside each other, this harmony coincides with an eerie fog said to be created by the she-dragon, Querig. As the fog unfurls itself over settlements, villagers forget their life histories until the past becomes as insubstantial as a half-remembered dream. It is within this setting that Ishiguro places his protagonists, Axl and Beatrice. A long-married elderly couple, they decide to leave their village in order to find their son before the mist causes them to forget him altogether. On their quest through lands inhabited by ogres, the couple face a number of frightening encounters. As well as a knight-errant, they meet mad monks, evil pixies and, most disturbing of all, a boatman who ferries people to the island of the dead. When the boatman explains that he only allows couples who are truly devoted to each other to travel across together, Axl and Beatrice start to worry that they will fail the boatman's test when the time comes. While fearing that their amnesia may cause them to forget how much they love each other, they also secretly worry that, if their memory returns, they may recall something about their relationship that they would rather forget. This sense of unease is exacerbated by vague memories of a quarrel and Axl's intermittent recollections of a former life as a warrior.

As fantasy tends to be a genre that 'serious' writers shy away from, many readers were surprised when Ishiguro's long-awaited follow-up to *Never Let Me Go* turned out to be a tale of giants and dragons. In writing *The Buried Giant*, however, the author has proved that it is not genre that makes literary fiction but the quality of the writing. Ishiguro incorporates a mix of literary influences, including a hint of *Beowulf* and more than a dash of *The Lord of the Rings*, to create a haunting story which pulls the reader along in a strange sort of reverie. Beatrice and Axl's quest sensitively explores mortality and the pain of loss that inevitably accompanies love. On a wider level, their story, set within an era when native Britons fought invading Saxons, is a metaphor for the way humans respond to atrocities through history. By laying out the pros and cons of remembering, he examines the conflict between the duty to remember and the desire to forget.

ABOUT THE AUTHOR

Kazuo Ishiguro was born in 1954 in Nagasaki, Japan. He and his family moved to Britain in 1960 when his father took a research post at the National Institute of Oceanography. Ishiguro was educated at a boys' grammar school in Surrey. Before enrolling at the University of Kent, where he studied English and Philosophy, he took a gap year, working as a grouse-beater for the Queen Mother at Balmoral while trying to make it as a recording artist. After graduating he worked as a social worker in Glasgow and London and then embarked on a creative writing MA at the University of East Anglia. His first novel, *A Pale View of Hills,* was published in 1982 and, the following year, he appeared on *Granta* magazine's 20 Best of Young British Writers list. Subsequent novels include *An Artist of the Floating World; The Remains of the Day; The Unconsoled; When We Were Orphans,* and *Never Let Me Go. The Remains of the Day* won the Booker Prize for Fiction and both this novel and *Never Let Me Go* have been made into movies. He has also written a number of short stories and screenplays.

Ishiguro's novels have become known for their unpredictable genres and subject matter. He has tackled historical fiction, the detective novel, speculative fiction and, most recently, fantasy. While some of his works address his Japanese ancestry, others are very British. He was awarded the OBE in 1995 for services to literature and currently lives in London with his wife and daughter.

IN A NUTSHELL

A haunting fantasy novel exploring love, loss and the importance of memory

THEMES

History; amnesia; memory; loss; love; mortality; guilt; concealment

DISCUSSION QUESTIONS

1/ Ishiguro's novels have spanned a surprising range of genres, from period romance (*The Remains of the Day*), to the detective novel (*We were Orphans*) to dystopian science fiction (*Never Let Me Go*). Were you surprised to discover that the author's most recent novel takes the form of a fantasy quest? Can a fictional world inhabited by ogres and pixies be considered as serious literary fiction? Would you normally choose to read fantasy fiction?

2/ *The Buried Giant* plays with the traditional genre of the quest. Like many quest heroes, Axl and Beatrice embark on a dangerous journey with a particular goal in mind. What other elements of the story conform to our expectations of the quest genre and in what ways does Ishiguro depart from them? Does the goal of the quest change as the novel progresses?

3/ When Kazuo Ishiguro presented the first draft of *The Buried Giant* to his wife, she criticised its overly archaic and flowery language. As a result, the author began the novel again in a much plainer style. Did you feel the pared down language of the finished novel worked? What effect does it have on the feel of the narrative?

4/ The buried giant of the novel's title and the mist that lingers over the land are both images of concealment: an important theme in the novel. In what ways do Ishiguro's characters deceive each other and also themselves. What are they hiding and why?

5/ In previous novels Ishiguro has always chosen to use a first person narrator to tell his story. In *The Buried Giant*, he deliberately departs from this style, using a third person narrator who is occasionally interrupted by the first person voices of the characters. Compare the first person narrative sections with those by the third person narrator. How do they differ in their effect? Why do you think Ishiguro chose a mixture of the two styles for this particular story?

6/ *The Buried Giant* is set in a period of historical limbo, just after the Romans departed from England and before the Anglo-Saxons fully settled. Why do you think Ishiguro chose this blank period in English history as a backdrop to his story?

7/ Beatrice and Axl survive a number of grotesque encounters on their travels. Which did you find the most disturbing and why?

8/ When Gawain leads Beatrice, Axl and Edwin through the underground tunnel beneath the monastery, each of them sees a different vision. Do you think the sightings are real or imagined? What do these visions say about them as individuals?

9/ Discuss the relationship between Wistan and Edwin. What do you think it is that they seek from each other? Is Edwin a born warrior, as Wistan suggests, or is he simply shaped to fulfil this role? How did you interpret Edwin's belief that his mother's voice still speaks to him?

10/ For much of the novel the aged Arthurian knight, Sir Gawain, is portrayed as almost comical in his ineffectiveness. Does our perception of him alter as the novel progresses and, if so, why?

11/ Beatrice and Axl share a loving marriage, although Axl occasionally fears that he may have done something in the past to blight their happiness. Did the revelation of Beatrice's adultery come as a shock? Did you reassess her character in the light of it?

12/ The novel ends with the expectation that, as the mist evaporates and memory is restored to the people of England, violence will soon erupt between the Britons and the Saxons. Do you believe Wistan's decision to kill Querig is the right one, or do you side with Sir Gawain's belief that protection of the dragon is necessary in the interests of peace? Is Wistan motivated by the desire to restore truth, or a vengeful urge to awaken ill-feeling between the Britons and the Saxons? With real historical genocides in mind (e.g. those in Rwanda, Srebrenica or the Holocaust) discuss whether historical amnesia is sometimes necessary for communities to move on after great trauma. Should justice sometimes be abandoned in order to break the cycle of violence, or is remembrance more important?

13/ Many of the questions raised about collective memory in the novel are also relevant to Beatrice and Axl's marriage. Do you think their relationship has suffered or benefited from their amnesia? Is their love less authentic because they cannot remember the sorrows of their past, or is forgetting an essential part of the survival of love?

14/ One of Ishiguro's aims in *The Buried Giant* was to celebrate the things that are important to people when death approaches. How does this theme of mortality emerge in the novel? What does the boatman represent and why does Beatrice become so preoccupied with the questions he is likely to ask them? How did you interpret the final scene where Beatrice journeys to the island alone? Discuss Beatrice and Axl's reactions to their final separation.

15/ Why did Ishiguro choose to write the last chapter of his novel from the perspective of the boatman? Is he a sympathetic character or simply an unfeeling arbiter of death?

FURTHER READING

Never Let Me Go, Kazuo Ishiguro
The Chimes, Anna Smaill
The Unlikely Pilgrimage of Harold Fry, Rachel Joyce
The Road, Cormac McCarthy
The Lord of the Rings, J.R.R. Tolkien

COMPARE & CONTRAST TO

The Heart Goes Last. Discuss the similarities and differences between the journeys taken by married couples Beatrix and Axl and Charmaine and Stan.

The Catcher in the Rye
by J.D. Salinger

FIRST PUBLISHED

1951

LENGTH

198 pages

SETTING

New York, late 1940s/early 1950s

ABOUT THE BOOK

The Catcher in the Rye needs little introduction. It is, without doubt, one of the best-known classic American novels. It has also attained the dual, contradictory honours of appearing on banned book lists, as well as becoming a standard set text for English literature classes. Since its first publication in 1951, J.D. Salinger's novel has never been out of print and has achieved global sales of over 65 million copies.

So, what is the secret of the novel's staying power? As far as plot goes, there isn't a great deal of action. The book's seventeen-year-old narrator, Holden Caulfield, remembers events from the previous year. During this forty-eight-hour period, Holden was expelled from his expensive prep school and, before returning home to face the wrath of his parents, checked into a New York hotel while trying to make contact with old friends and acquaintances. This unremarkable sounding story, however, is significantly related from the confines of a psychiatric hospital and, through Holden's various encounters, the reader begins to understand the nature of the narrator's psychological conflict.

Holden's cynical narrative voice, although peppered with the teen jargon of the time, is timeless, capturing the very essence of teenage alienation and angst. Teetering on the edge of adulthood, he longs to return to the innocence of childhood. Holden's voice speaks down the years to any reader who is undergoing adolescence or still remembers the tortures of their teenage years. For those who first experienced *The Catcher in the Rye* as an adolescent, either as a personal read or a school set text, it is a particularly rich novel to return to for book group discussion. Did you react to the novel in the same way second time around? Are there elements of the novel which can only be appreciated with age and experience? And does your group agree that this slim volume still deserves its place in the literary hall of fame? Responses to these questions are sure to be divided, as are reactions to Holden, who readers tend to adore or violently dislike, with little in between.

ABOUT THE AUTHOR

Jerome David Salinger was born in 1919 in New York. At college he began to write short stories, some of which appeared in *The New Yorker*. As his writing career started to take off, Salinger was drafted into the army to fight in World Word II. During his time in active service, he survived a number of notoriously bloody conflicts (including the D-Day landings) and witnessed the liberation of concentration camps. While fighting in the war, he also wrote some of the material that would later be used in *The Catcher in the Rye*. The war took its toll, however, and when Salinger returned to civilian life he suffered a nervous breakdown. When *The Catcher in the Rye* was published in 1951, he was unprepared for the scale of its success and became one of the most famous of literary recluses, rarely granting interviews or making public appearances. Despite only publishing one full-length novel he is considered one of the most influential American writers of the twentieth century.

IN A NUTSHELL

An iconic fictional account of the painful transition from childhood to adulthood

THEMES

Teenage angst; alienation; loneliness; innocence vs. corruption; authenticity; loss

DISCUSSION QUESTIONS

1/ Holden Caulfield is one of the best-known characters from twentieth century fiction. What is it that makes him so memorable? What is distinctive about his narrative voice? Is he a reliable narrator?

2/ Readers are often divided over Holden - some adore him, others find him irritating. How did you feel about him? Do you think Salinger wanted the reader to like him?

3/ Holden values authenticity and despises anything he believes to be "phoney". What does he think of as authentic and who and what does he accuse of phoniness? Are his assessments always accurate? Are there instances when Holden himself could justifiably be described as phoney?

4/ Holden confides to Phoebe that he wants to be a 'catcher in the rye'. What does he mean by this and how is this ambition demonstrated in his anxieties and actions?

5/ Holden largely divides the world into two camps - innocent children and corrupt adults. Are Holden's notions about the purity of childhood overly simplistic? Do you think the divide between childhood and adulthood is as wide as he perceives it to be? Which camp does Holden himself fall into?

6/ Much of Holden's inner conflict centres upon his feelings about the opposite sex. Think about his experiences with Jane Gallagher, Sally Hayes, Sunny and the women in the Lavender Room. How do his feelings about Jane differ from those inspired by the other women? Why does he feel bad about this? Can much of Holden's inner turmoil be explained by raging hormones?

7/ Holden takes great pride in his red hunting cap. What is its significance?

8/ Holden feels a sense of alienation and the novel is structured around his attempts to connect with both friends and strangers. Discuss the different types of connections Holden attempts to make with other people in the novel. Why is intimacy so elusive? Does the problem lie with Holden or those he tries to communicate with?

9/ Although Salinger's novel is immensely poignant, it is also shot through with a great deal of humour. Was there a particular comic episode or piece of dialogue that really stood out for you?

10/ Why, at the end of the novel, is Holden so moved at the sight of Phoebe on the carousel? How does this scene echo his earlier thoughts about the glass cases in the museum? What is the significance of the gold ring the children reach for, and how did you interpret Holden's reaction to this?

11/ Salinger's novel is a coming-of-age story – a genre which conventionally follows the protagonist from innocence and inexperience to a deeper knowledge of the self and the world. Does *The Catcher in the Rye* follow the conventions of this genre? How, if at all, does Holden change or develop?

12/ The Principal of Pencey Prep compares life to "a game" and advises Holden that he must learn to "play it according to the rules." At what points in the novel does Holden display his inability to follow life's "rules"? Would learning to play by the rules make him a better or happier person?

13/ Many readers first experience *The Catcher in the Rye* as young adults and then return to it in later life. Have you read the novel before? If so, is it best appreciated in adolescence or with the experience of age? Is it as relevant to women as it is to men?

14/ When *The Catcher in the Rye* was first published in 1951, Holden Caulfield's non-conformist attitude and use of teenage vernacular caught the spirit of the age, as young people rebelled against the conservatism of the 1940s. Do you think teenagers of today can still identify with Holden? Do you think the novel's popularity as a set high school text discourages young people from reading it for pleasure?

15/ In 1951, *The Christian Science Monitor* declared that *The Catcher in the Rye* was "not fit for children to read" and the novel remains near the top of the list of banned books in public libraries in certain areas of the USA. Mark David Chapman also cited Salinger's novel as influential in his decision to murder John Lennon. Why do you think the novel provokes such powerful reactions?

FURTHER READING

The Adventures of Huckleberry Finn, Mark Twain
To Kill a Mockingbird, Harper Lee
Black Swan Green, David Mitchell
Dodgers, Bill Beverly
The Bell Jar, Sylvia Plath

COMPARE & CONTRAST TO

The Shock of the Fall and *We Were Liars* for its distinctive teenage narrative voice and exploration of the agonies of adolescence

Everything I Never Told You
by Celeste Ng

FIRST PUBLISHED

2014

LENGTH

304 pages

SETTING

1970s Ohio

ABOUT THE BOOK

Middlewood is a small college town where nothing much happens. That is until one spring day in 1977, when 16-year-old Lydia Lee goes missing and her body is subsequently found in Middlewood Lake. Lydia was one of the last girls anyone would expect to get into trouble. The favourite child of both James Lee, a Chinese American professor of history, and his wife, Marilyn, a Harvard-educated homemaker, Lydia was responsible, hard-working and eager to please. The circumstances surrounding her death, however, raise questions over whether it can be a straightforward case of accidental drowning. Why, for example, did she risk rowing herself to the middle of the lake when she could not swim? What are her siblings, Hannah and Nath, holding back from their parents? And why is Nath convinced that their neighbour, Jack, had something to do with Lydia's death? As surprising details about her life and death emerge, the Lees are forced to reassess their relationship with Lydia and acknowledge that they did not really know her at all.

While this kind of plot may sound familiar, *Everything I Never Told You* is far more sophisticated than your average thriller. The author takes the mystery of Lydia's death and uses it to slowly peel away the facade of a Chinese American family who appear to be living the American Dream. Although set in the 1970s, many of the racial issues it explores are sadly still relevant to Asian Americans and other mixed race families today. The Lees encounter many different forms of racial prejudice and stereotyping, from the subtle to the overt, and every one of these incidents was directly inspired by something that happened to the author or someone she knows. The feeling of standing outside of two cultures, rather than fitting in with both, is also something members of mixed race families may still be all too familiar with. Lydia's story painfully illustrates that even the apparently complimentary perception of Asians as a 'model minority' comes with its own pressures.

Above all, Ng's novel is a profoundly sensitive exploration of family dynamics. By providing the perspective of each member of the Lee family, the narrative is equally sympathetic to the conflicts of both parents and children. Many readers, while not necessarily approving of Marilyn and James's behaviour, will sympathise with their desire for their children to be successful and popular. Parents of older children will also relate to the novel's underlying message: that we never truly know our offspring. The moment when Marilyn breaks the locks on Lydia's diaries, only to find that they are completely blank, is a chilling representation of this uncomfortable fact. Meanwhile, our hearts go out to Lydia, whose desperate desire to please her parents means that she cannot be honest with them. The things that are 'never told' in the novel relate not only to the secrets surrounding Lydia's drowning but the silences and repressions that occur within many family units.

ABOUT THE AUTHOR

Celeste Ng (pronounced "-ing") is a Chinese American writer who was born in the USA. Originally from Hong Kong, Celeste's parents moved to the Midwest of the USA in the late 1960s: her father was a NASA physicist and her mother a chemist. Celeste grew up in a largely white community and was the only Asian in her school in Pittsburgh. She studied English at Harvard University and then earned an MFA in creative writing from the University of Michigan where she won the Hopwood Award. Before the publication of her debut novel, *Everything I Never Told You*, Celeste's essays and short stories had appeared in a number of publications. *Everything I Never Told You* was voted Amazon's #1 Best Book of 2014 and won the Massachusetts Book Award, the Asian/Pacific American Award for Literature and the Medici Book Club Prize. The author currently lives in Cambridge, Massachusetts with her husband and son.

IN A NUTSHELL

A poignant mystery exploring mixed race identity and family dynamics

THEMES

Chinese American identity; racism; women's gender roles; belonging; parent/child & sibling relationships; loss; secrecy; repression; grief; loneliness

DISCUSSION QUESTIONS

1/ At the beginning of the novel the omniscient narrator reveals that Lydia is dead before her family make the discovery. Why do you think the author chooses to reveal this information so quickly? How does she still manage to build suspense in the narrative?

2/ Lydia is the favourite child of both James and Marilyn. Why is this? Is being perceived as 'the golden child' a blessing or a curse for Lydia? How does it affect her siblings? In your own experience is parental favouritism inexcusable or inevitable?

3/ How do Marilyn and James's aspirations for Lydia differ? How do these aspirations relate to their own thwarted hopes and desires? Is it a natural instinct to want our children to succeed where we feel we have failed?

4/ Marilyn's discovery that Lydia's diaries are full of "obstinate silence" highlights how scarily unknowable the lives of teenagers can be. Discuss the lengths Lydia goes to in order to hide her failures and unhappiness. Do you think her parents should have guessed that something was amiss?

5/ The novel's title refers not only to the things that Lydia doesn't tell her parents but also to the secrets the rest of the Lee family keep from each other. Discuss the things that they hide from each other. What are their motivations for doing so?

6/ Discuss the way the 'Marco Polo' incident sums up James's complex feelings about Nath. How did you feel about the way James handled the situation? What would you have done in his position?

7/ What is it that attracts Marilyn and James to each other? Is this a sufficient foundation to build a marriage upon?

8/ When Marilyn reveals that she is to marry James, her mother predicts that she will regret the decision as society will not accept them as a couple and their children will suffer. How accurate does this prediction turn out to be? Should Marilyn have heeded her mother's advice?

9/ Discuss the different kinds of racial prejudice and stereotyping faced by the Lee family. Do you think Chinese stereotypes have changed since the 1970s?

10/ What does her mother's cookbook represent to Marilyn? What role does cooking in general play in the novel?

11/ How does Lydia's death relate to Marilyn's disappearance over a decade earlier? What impact does Marilyn's brief absence have upon the family dynamics?

12/ Discuss the prejudice Marilyn encounters as a woman in a man's world. Why does she eventually give up her professional ambitions? Did you agree with her conclusion that it is impossible for a woman to balance her family and professional life? How does the lifestyle of Jack Wolff's mother prove or disprove this theory?

13/ James's moral code often leaves a lot to be desired – from his reluctance to be seen with his parents to his affair with Louisa Chen. Did you find him a sympathetic character?

14/ By continually shifting the narrative's perspective, the author gives readers insight into the minds of each member of the Lee family. Overall, did you identify more with the parents or the children?

15/ Why do you think the author chose to set the novel in the 1970s? Are there any aspects of the book that would not be credible if placed in a contemporary context?

FURTHER READING

What the Dead Know, Laura Lippman
Amy and Isabelle, Elizabeth Strout
The Love Wife, Gish Jen
All My Puny Sorrows, Miriam Toews
We Need To Talk About Kevin, Lionel Shriver

COMPARE & CONTRAST TO

The Husband's Secret for its exploration of family secrets and *The Sympathizer* for its examination of Asian stereotyping in the USA

The Fault in Our Stars
by John Green

FIRST PUBLISHED

2012

LENGTH

332 pages

SETTING

Indiana and Amsterdam

ABOUT THE BOOK

16-year-old Hazel Grace Lancaster lives in Indiana and has stage IV thyroid cancer. After almost dying when she was 14, she was given a trial drug which successfully shrunk her tumours. Since then, Hazel's cancer has shown no signs of spreading but the 'miracle' drug has not cured her. Requiring a portable oxygen tank to help her breathe wherever she goes, she lives in a continual state of uncertainty about her life expectancy. Concerned that their daughter is becoming reclusive and may be depressed, Hazel's parents urge her to attend a weekly support group for young cancer victims. Hazel agrees but finds the regularly "rotating" cast depressing until a handsome 17-year-old boy joins its ranks. Gus Waters attends the group to support his friend, Isaac, who has eye cancer. Formerly a talented basketball player, Gus is an amputee who had osteosarcoma in his leg but has now been declared cancer-free. Hazel and Gus's flirtatious friendship soon blossoms into love. In the background, however, the spectre of Hazel's illness looms over the young lovers.

The Fault in Our Stars flew to the #1 spot in the New York Times bestsellers list on publication and was adapted into a major motion picture. Despite this, some readers are reluctant to give it a go. For those who like their fiction to be life-affirming, a story about a teenage girl with cancer may not be particularly appealing. The key to the novel's success is that it defies many readers' preconceptions about 'sick-lit' (the recent trend for young adult fiction dealing with subjects such as disability, terminal illness and suicide). The narrator, Hazel, is in fact scornful of many of the cancer novel conventions, e.g. the portrayal of a stock character whose courage never wavers through the pain and indignity of cancer. Hazel's viewpoint is utterly honest, irreverent and often very funny.

In terms of genre, *The Fault in Our Stars* is hard to define. Rather than a young adult novel about cancer it is perhaps more accurate to describe it as a coming-of-age rom-com, complicated by the issues of terminal illness. John Green felt that many books portraying cancer in teenagers celebrate the characters' courage at the expense of depicting them as real people. To redress the balance, he wanted to write a novel that would humanise them. He is therefore careful not to define his characters by their illness, instead delivering vivid, memorable teenagers who also have cancer. Having said this, the novel never makes light of its subject matter. Green sensitively explores the emotions of those who face impending death and also those who know they will be left behind to grieve. A tragi-comedy, the novel tackles life and loss, but with the emphasis firmly upon life.

ABOUT THE AUTHOR

John Green was born in 1977 and grew up in Orlando, Florida. Before becoming a full-time writer he worked as a publishing assistant and production editor for *Booklist Magazine*. He also spent some time as a chaplain in a children's hospital where he became friends with Esther Earl, a 16-year-old girl who died of thyroid cancer. Green acknowledges that getting to know Esther largely inspired *The Fault in Our Stars*.

The Fault in Our Stars took Green a decade to write and is his fourth novel aimed at the young adult market. Prior to the hugely successful reception of *The Fault in Our Stars*, Green had already been the recipient of the Michael L. Printz award and had won an Edgar award for his young adult fiction. His previous novels are *Looking for Alaska*, *An Abundance of Katherines* and *Paper Towns*.

In addition to his high profile as a writer, John Green has

gained international recognition as one of the "vlogbrothers". In 2007 he and his brother, Hank, began to post one another video blogs on YouTube. The videos soon gained popularity and spawned an online community calling themselves 'nerd fighters'. Nerd fighters seek to popularise intellectualism and generally make the world a nicer place. Their achievements have included raising funds to fight poverty and planting thousands of trees around the world. Green has over one million followers on Twitter and makes himself accessible to fans, frequently answering questions about his work.

IN A NUTSHELL

A moving rom-com tackling the sensitive subject of teenage terminal illness

THEMES

Mortality; cancer; adolescence; illness and identity; love and loss

DISCUSSION QUESTIONS

1/ Discuss the ways the combined conditions of cancer and adolescence affect the experiences of Hazel, Gus and Isaac.

2/ John Green's decision to make his protagonist a teenage girl is brave and unusual for a male author. Did you find Hazel's voice and her thought processes convincing?

3/ *The Fault in Our Stars* explores the pain of parents whose children are terminally ill. Discuss the way Hazel and Gus's parents deal with their child's illness.

4/ The romance between Hazel and Gus is a classic example of opposites attracting. Discuss their contrasting attitudes to life and death. What do they gain from each other? Do you think their relationship had the potential to last?

5/ Why does Hazel become so emotionally invested in *An Imperial Affliction*? Why is she so eager to find out what happens to the characters after the novel's abrupt ending?

6/ Hazel believes that most novels about cancer "suck". Do you agree? Would you ordinarily choose to read a book on this subject? Did *The Fault in our Stars* differ from your expectations of the genre? Would you be tempted to read other novels on the subject?

7/ Hazel, Gus and Isaac all indulge in gallows humour. Why do you think this is? Did the humour work for you or did it make you feel uncomfortable?

8/ In different ways Hazel and Gus both search for meaning in the face of death. Do you think they find it?

9/ Peter Van Houten suggests that grief does not change us but rather reveals our true selves. Do you think this is true? How is this revealed in the various characters' responses to grief?

10/ Discuss the changes Gus undergoes over the course of the novel. Are there differences between the personas of 'Augustus' and 'Gus'?

11/ One of the great charms of this novel is the witty dialogue between Hazel and Gus. Did you find their exchanges realistic, or are they simply too clever to be credible? If they are somewhat unrepresentative of the average teenager's conversation, does this matter?

12/ Did you suspect that Gus was the "grenade" rather than Hazel? Discuss how the dynamics of Hazel and Gus's relationship change when Hazel discovers this.

13/ When Hazel meets her literary hero, Peter Van Houten, she is devastated to discover that the man who wrote such a moving novel is a selfish alcoholic. Do you think it is necessary to be a good person in order to write compassionate fiction? Have you ever met one of your idols and been disappointed?

14/ The ending of *The Fault in Our Stars* leaves the reader uncertain of Hazel's fate. Is John Green, like Peter Van Houten, guilty of leaving his readership hanging? What was your overall feeling after finishing the novel? Did you find it depressing, uplifting, or somewhere in between?

15/ *The Fault in Our Stars* was marketed as a Young Adult novel. Do you think this is an appropriate literary category to place it in? Why, or why not?

FURTHER READING

A Monster Calls, Patrick Ness
Me and Earl and the Dying Girl, Jesse Andrews
Grace Williams Says It Loud, Emma Henderson
Eleanor and Park, Rainbow Rowell
Me Before You, Jojo Moyes

COMPARE & CONTRAST TO

The Shock of the Fall for its depiction of an adolescence tainted by illness and the impact upon family.

The Girl on the Train
by Paula Hawkins

FIRST PUBLISHED

2015

LENGTH

320 pages

SETTING

London, England

ABOUT THE BOOK

The premise behind *The Girl on the Train* is simple but brilliant. What if a London commuter, accustomed to staring at the same view through the train window each day, unexpectedly witnesses something shocking? And what if it becomes clear that the sighting is directly related to the mysterious disappearance of a young woman? Paula Hawkins makes this idea more interesting still by creating an unreliable narrator. Rachel, the commuter in question, is far from a dispassionate observer of events. With her own personal life in tatters, she has become fixated with the perfect-looking couple who occupy one of the houses that backs on to the railway tracks. Nicknaming them 'Jess and Jason', Rachel fantasises about the details of their golden lives. Her emotional investment in the couple means that she is horrified when she spots Jess (aka Megan Hipwell) kissing a man who is not Jason. Her shock and disbelief intensify when, a few days later, it emerges that Megan has suspiciously vanished and that her husband appears to be the number one suspect. Rachel becomes convinced that she holds the key to unlocking the mystery of Megan's disappearance. Her ability to solve it, however, is frustratingly hampered by her fragile emotional state, lack of objectivity and alcohol-induced blackouts.

Written through the alternating perspectives of three complex and troubled women, this intelligent psychological thriller focuses on the dark side of human nature and provides great material for book group discussion. Hyped as the British *Gone Girl*, Hawkins' novel shares many of the traits of Gillian Flynn's bestseller, including a missing woman, an untrustworthy female protagonist and the portrayal of a dysfunctional marriage. Like *Gone Girl*, the plot also raises some uncomfortable questions for readers to mull over: When does marital disharmony cross into the territory of domestic violence? When does a 'drinker' become a 'drunk'? And is it possible, or even desirable, for us ever to truly know one another?

ABOUT THE AUTHOR

Paula Hawkins was born and raised in Harare, Zimbabwe. She moved to London with her family when she was seventeen and has lived there ever since. After studying Economics, Politics and Philosophy at Oxford University, Hawkins became a journalist, specialising in business and finance and writing for a variety of publications, including *The Times*. Her career as a fiction writer began with the publication of *Confessions of a Reluctant Recessionista*, a romantic comedy written under the pen name Amy Silver. Three further Amy Silver novels followed but Hawkins became increasingly aware that 'chick lit' was not her natural genre. *The Girl on the Train* marked Hawkins' debut into the territory of the psychological thriller, inspired by her own experience of commuting into London for years. When Hawkins's literary agent sent the still half-finished novel out to publishers, a bidding war erupted as editors spotted the potential of *The Girl on the Train* to become the hot new psychological thriller. As predicted, the novel was an immediate commercial and critical success, soaring to the top of the *New York Times* bestsellers list and being quickly optioned by Dreamworks for a film adaptation.

IN A NUTSHELL

A claustrophobic tale of obsession, amnesia and murder

THEMES

Identity; deception; loneliness; domestic violence; women's gender roles; alcoholism

DISCUSSION QUESTIONS

1/ What lies behind Rachel's interest in 'Jason and Jess'? How do her imaginings compare with reality and what does this say about our perceptions of other people? What other misconceptions about identity are exposed in the novel?

2/ Did you enjoy the use of alternating viewpoints in the novel? Why do you think the author chose to use this technique and what did it add to the story? Why does Hawkins wait until halfway through the novel to introduce Anna's perspective?

3/ Rachel, Megan and Anna all display unsympathetic or socially unacceptable character traits. Discuss what these traits are. Would they have the same impact if they were displayed by a male character? Which character did you most sympathise with?

4/ Deception is a recurrent theme in the novel. Discuss the lies the characters tell each other and themselves and their reasons for doing so. In what ways are couples shown to collude with each other's lies? Is it sometimes necessary in a relationship to ignore or pretend to believe a lie?

5/ Why do Megan and Rachel both become fixated with Kamal Abdic? What did you make of him as a character?

6/ Rachel suggests that society only values women for "their looks and their role as mothers." Do you think this is true? How is Rachel's claim borne out by the experiences of the female characters in the novel?

7/ The vulnerability of young children is emphasised in the death of Megan's first baby and in the incident where Rachel snatches Evie. How did you feel about the circumstances surrounding the death of Megan's baby? Was she right to feel responsible? What do you think Rachel's intentions were when she took Evie?

8/ Discuss the symbolism of the train and its tracks in the novel. What does it mean to Rachel, Megan and Anna respectively?

9/ Kamal Abdic defines Scott's habitual invasion of Megan's privacy as "emotional abuse". Is he right, or do you think Megan's untrustworthy behaviour justifies the way Scott checks up on her? What would you do in his position?

10/ Hawkins sought to demonstrate in her novel that the majority of people who encounter violence do so in a domestic setting. Discuss the way that the author juxtaposes images of domesticity with violence. Is this representation of domesticity a skewed one, or disturbingly accurate?

11/ Although set in the bustling city of London, where people are forced into close proximity with one another, the novel explores the difficulty of forging meaningful human relationships. Discuss the themes of loneliness and isolation in the novel.

12/ Through the character of Rachel, the author explores the devastating effects of alcoholism. Discuss the different ways that Rachel's excessive drinking impacts on her life. Did you sympathise with her or feel frustrated by her inability to stop drinking? Do you think it is true that there is a fine line between "a drinker" and "a drunk"? Is alcoholism more shocking in a female character than a male and, if so, why?

13/ Parts of *The Girl on the Train* have a strong cinematic feel and the novel was quickly adapted into a film. Did any episodes in particular strike you as more cinematic than literary? If so, which ones and why?

14/ Did the novel's conclusion surprise you and did you find it satisfying? How do you foresee the future for Rachel and Anna?

15/ Pre-release publicity for *The Girl on the Train* compared the novel to *Gone Girl*. For those who have read Gillian Flynn's bestselling thriller, what are the similarities between the two novels and what are the differences? Which did you prefer?

FURTHER READING

Elizabeth is Missing, Emma Healey
Before I Go to Sleep, S.J. Watson
How to be a Good Wife, Emma Chapman
Notes on a Scandal, Zoe Heller
Strangers on a Train, Patricia Highsmith

COMPARE & CONTRAST TO

Gone Girl (which is the more enjoyable thriller and why?) and *We Were Liars* for the authors' use of memory loss as a plot device

The Girls
by Emma Cline

FIRST PUBLISHED

2016

LENGTH

368 pages

SETTING

California – 1969 and the present day

ABOUT THE BOOK

One of the most anticipated debut novels of 2016, *The Girls* was the subject of a bidding war between twelve publishing houses. In the end its 27-year-old author, Emma Cline, reportedly accepted a $2 million, three-book publishing deal from Random House. The novel provoked such excitement for two reasons: its author was already a prize-winning short story writer and its story was inspired by the notorious Charles Manson murders. In 1969, female members of Charles Manson's 'Family' killed Roman Polanski's pregnant wife, along with friends of the couple who were staying at the film director's home. *The Girls* is Cline's fictional interpretation of what might have compelled the female members of Manson's cult to commit such an atrocity.

The story is told from the perspective of middle-aged Evie Boyd, who is staying at a friend's empty house while waiting for her next live-in care job. Evie's solitude is unexpectedly interrupted by the arrival of her friend's son, Julian, with his girlfriend, Sasha. Observing the disrespectful way Julian treats Sasha triggers Evie's memories of the summer of 1969 and the narrative shifts back in time. At the age of fourteen, Evie is waiting to be packed off to boarding school when term recommences. While her father has moved away with his young girlfriend, Evie's mother has started dating again. Evie tries to enliven her days by licking batteries with her best friend, Connie, but what she really longs for is for someone to notice and love her. When Evie's relationship with Connie turns sour, she begins to feel that she does not belong anywhere. That is, until she spots 19-year old Suzanne, the most charismatic member of 'the Girls', who live in a commune at a local ranch. Attracted by Suzanne's air of glamour and the camaraderie of the Girls, Evie begins to visit the commune more and more frequently. While the other girls there are captivated by the group's leader, Russell, Evie remains fixated on Suzanne. Believing that she and the older girl share a special bond, Evie ignores the signs that things are taking an increasingly nasty turn in the days leading up to a shocking murder.

While publicity has made the most of this novel's sensational real-life subject matter, Cline's fictionalised treatment of the story is remarkably intelligent and restrained. As the title suggests, the focus of the novel is not the Charles Manson-inspired cult leader, Russell, but the girls who fall under his manipulative spell. While Russell remains a rather pathetic figure in the shadows, Cline's focus is upon why the girls fall prey to his influence in the first place. At one point Evie suggests that it is simply "bad luck" that she became involved in Russell's group but Cline makes it clear that the real culprit is female conditioning. The relationship between Russell and his Girls is just an extreme example of the power imbalance evident in almost all of the male/female relationships in the novel. Such skewed power dynamics, Cline implies, are caused by a society in which girls are indoctrinated with the belief that they are incomplete without a man.

One of the most remarkable achievements of this novel is the way in which it captures the raw intensity of emotion only experienced in adolescence. Evie's self-consciousness, vulnerability and desperate longing to be loved will cause many a reader to wince and recall their own painful teenage years. Add to this the pressures that girls, in particular, are exposed to (objectification, sexual exploitation, powerlessness and humiliation) and, the author seems to suggest, it is unsurprising that some girls might be capable of murder.

*Contains explicit sexual content and some of the language is not for the easily offended.

ABOUT THE AUTHOR

Emma Cline grew up in Sonomo, California, and was fascinated by cults and communes even as a child. She graduated with an MFA in creative writing from Columbia University and was awarded the Plimpton Prize for Fiction for her short stories in 2014. She works as a reader for *The New Yorker* fiction department and *The Girls* is her debut novel.

IN A NUTSHELL

A raw and poetic portrait of adolescence and the way the world treats women in general

THEMES

The angst of adolescence; loneliness; belonging; the power dynamics between men and women; the social conditioning of girls

DISCUSSION QUESTIONS

1/ Why does the author choose to have Evie tell her story from the perspective of middle age? How does teenage Evie compare with middle-aged Evie? Is she a sympathetic character?

2/ Discuss the events leading up to Evie's first sighting of the Girls. How do these recent events make her more susceptible to their influence?

3/ Evie's first encounter with Julian and Sasha triggers her memories of 1969. What parallels does Evie see between Sasha and her own teenage self? Why does Evie confide in Sasha?

4/ As a teenager, Evie is presented with three adult role models - her mother, Tamar and Suzanne. How do these women differ and what do they have in common?

5/ The novel's critique of gender conditioning is neatly

summarised in Evie's observation: "All that time I had spent readying myself, the articles that taught me that life was really just a waiting room until someone notices you – the boys had spent that time becoming themselves." What hopes do the girls and women in the novel have of their relationships with men? How does the dream compare with the reality? Are girls still conditioned to believe that they are incomplete until they meet the right man, or have things moved on since the 1960s?

6/ Discuss the chain of power dynamics between Russell and the Girls, Evie and Suzanne, and Evie and Teddy. In each of these relationships, how is this power exerted?

7/ Discuss the uncomfortable tension in the novel between Evie's emerging sexuality and her sexual exploitation by older men. How does Evie feel after her first sexual experiences? Do you think her experience reflects that of many teenage girls?

8/ The novel features a number of absent parents (Evie's father, Connie's mother, Julian's father) and Evie assumes that if any of the Girls had caring parents they wouldn't be at the ranch. Do you think this is a fair judgement to make? Are Evie's or Julian's parents responsible for the paths their children take?

9/ In the *New York Times*, Dylan Landis observes that some of the sentences in *The Girls* are "so finely wrought that they could almost be worn as jewellery". Discuss the way Cline uses poetic language to describe dark and often unpleasant subject matter. Did you find the poetic tone of the novel effective?

10/ To what extent is Evie brainwashed by the members of the commune and to what extent does she deliberately turn a blind eye to what she doesn't want to see? At what point (if at all) does she realise that she has viewed the life there through rose-tinted glasses?

11/ Suzanne only decides not to involve Evie in the murders en route to the crime. What do you think changes her mind? Is her motive to protect Evie (as Evie likes to think) or something less noble?

12/ For the rest of her life Evie remains unsure whether she would have taken part in the murders, had she been there. Do you think she would have been capable of participating? Does Evie's last-minute removal from the situation make the narrative more interesting, or is it something of a cop out on the part of the author?

13/ After the murders Suzanne, in particular, is demonised by the press. Does she deserve to be perceived in this way? Do you think Cline suggests that there are extenuating circumstances for her actions? Why is murder considered more shocking when it is committed by a woman?

14/ Evie's observations on the ghoulish online forums devoted to Russell and the murders echo the real-life websites dedicated to Charles Manson and his Family. Do you think there is an unhealthy tendency to glamorise murder and violence in our society? Does Emma Cline manage to avoid this kind of glamorisation in her fictional retelling of the Charles Manson story?

15/ What is the significance of the stranger who approaches Evie at the end of the novel? Did you find the conclusion satisfying?

FURTHER READING

Mr Wroe's Virgins, Jane Rogers
The Bell Jar, Sylvia Plath
Imaginary Friends, Alison Lurie
Prep, Curtis Sittenfeld
The Outsiders, S.E. Hinton

COMPARE & CONTRAST TO

My Brilliant Friend for its exploration of the impact of gender expectations upon young women. *Station Eleven* for its depiction of the dynamics of cults, or *Room* for its fictional re-imagining of a shocking true crime

The Glorious Heresies
by Lisa McInerney

FIRST PUBLISHED

2015

LENGTH

384 pages

SETTING

Cork city, Ireland

ABOUT THE BOOK

Anyone who thinks of Ireland as a romantic land, rich in mists and lush green countryside, is in for a shock when they read *The Glorious Heresies*. Lisa McInerney's novel is certainly no tourist advert for the Emerald Isle. Instead, it offers a gritty portrayal of the underbelly of Irish urban life. The focus of the novel is Cork city, which remains devastated by the great Irish recession of 2008. A 'rotten' city, Cork offers its working-class inhabitants neither respectable ways to make a living nor spiritual comfort. In this landscape of seedy streets, doorways housing the homeless and run-down council estates, McInerney introduces her main characters. Ryan Cusack is a fifteen-year-old drug dealer; Ryan's father, Tony, is an abusive alcoholic; Jimmy Phelan is a gangland boss, recently reunited with his mother, Maureen, and, completing the cast is Georgie, a sex worker who once worked in the brothel that Jimmy has converted into a home for his mother. At the beginning of the novel, Ryan teeters on the threshold of manhood as he prepares to have sex with his girlfriend for the first time. Meanwhile, Maureen surveys the body of a burglar whom she has killed with a hefty religious piece of ornamentation. At first, the connection between the two stories is unclear. When Jimmy Phelan employs Tony

Cusack to dispose of the inconvenient corpse, however, it marks the beginning of a series of events that bring all five of the main characters together in a tangled web of coincidence.

While the plot of this novel revolves around an accidental murder, this is far from a traditional crime novel. There are no detectives in *The Glorious Heresies*. Neither is there any real threat that the crime will be discovered by the authorities. Instead the author explores the far-reaching consequences of Maureen's actions, which rumble on over the next five years. Through the perspectives of a number of characters, McInerney shows the ways their lives are changed by the death of one, seemingly inconsequential, man.

This novel is very likely to divide readers in a book club discussion and it is not for the easily offended. McInerney's text is liberally peppered with foul language, blasphemous curses and sexually explicit descriptions. Having said this, none of these features are used by the author for their shock value. Her aim is to create a realistic picture of the underclass of Irish society and polite vocabulary has no place here. Despite their frequent profanities, McInerney's characters are witty, perceptive and occasionally border on the poetic. They are also incredibly human. At one point, an omniscient narrator observes that, "Cork City isn't going to notice the last faltering steps of a lost little man … So scale it down. Zoom in. Look closer." This is precisely what the author does; focussing in on individuals we might normally choose to cross the street to avoid. By offering compassionate insights into the lives of drug dealers, addicts and sex workers, the novel makes it almost impossible for the reader not to sympathise with their moral conflicts. Although it seems inevitable, we cannot help hoping that sensitive teenager, Ryan, will buck the trend and avoid following in his father's footsteps. Meanwhile, Georgie's career as a prostitute is shown to be the result of a vicious, inescapable cycle. Even Jimmy Phelan, while not wholly sympathetic, tries to do right by his mother under very trying circumstances.

While investigating the moral dilemmas of her characters, McInerney manages to touch on a dizzying number of themes. As well as universal themes such as atonement, salvation, shame, and the fine line between vice and virtue, the author investigates class, poverty, Catholic doctrine, the desensitising effects of TV/video game violence, and the role of the internet in a sick society.

Perhaps the most important thing to emphasise about *The Glorious Heresies*, however is that it is very funny indeed. Like a literary version of 'Pulp Fiction', the novel is packed with brilliant one-liners as well as blackly comic incidents. I defy anyone to read the passage where Maureen confesses her crime to a Catholic priest, only to get into an argument with him about her vulgar language, without chuckling. It takes a very clever writer to make bleak subject matter so entertaining.

ABOUT THE AUTHOR

Lisa McInerney is an Irish writer and was born in 1981. In 2006 she started writing a regular blog about working-class life on a Galway council estate. McInerney churned out 'Arse End of Ireland' five times a week (written under the online persona 'Sweary Lady') while working as a receptionist and bringing up her young daughter. The raw talent in these blogs was recognised when she won the best humour prize at the Irish Blog Awards in 2009.

Although she wrote her first novel (about a magical horse) when she was eight years old, *The Glorious Heresies* was McInerney's first published novel. It was named Book of the Year by *The Irish Times*, *Sunday Independent* and *Sunday Business Post*. It also won the 2016 Baileys Women's Prize for Fiction and the Desmond Elliott prize. The author lives in Galway with her husband, daughter and dog and is currently working on a "loose sequel" to *The Glorious Heresies* which will continue the story of Ryan Cusack.

IN A NUTSHELL

A compassionate and humorous insight into the darker side of Irish society. Not for the easily offended!

THEMES

Poverty; class; addiction; violence; shame; the Catholic Church; virtue; corruption; redemption

DISCUSSION QUESTIONS

1/ Lisa McInerney has said that when her novel was first

published, "a few people thought it necessary to tell me how 'male' it was". Do you feel that *The Glorious Heresies* bears many of the hallmarks of a male writer? Do you associate certain qualities with novels written by women, or are there no differences between male and female texts?

2/ Did you enjoy the black humour in *The Glorious Heresies*? Did any passages in particular stand out for you? Is the humour necessary in order to make the subject matter bearable to read?

3/ *The Glorious Heresies* is littered with the dialect of Cork city. Did the use of Irish idiom enhance your reading experience or detract from it?

4/ Lisa McInerney describes her novel as a "breakneck and rowdy thing". Did the frantic pace and constant changes in narrative viewpoint work for you?

5/ The plot of the novel revolves around Maureen's murder of Robbie O'Sullivan and Jimmy's increasingly desperate attempts to contain her actions. Discuss Maureen's character and her increasingly unpredictable behaviour. Do you think there is any truth in Georgie's assessment of her as "a seer"?

6/ Discuss the way the novel critiques the doctrine of the Catholic Church. How do the experiences of Maureen, Georgie and Karine, who all experience unplanned pregnancies, sit with the Catholic reverence of the Virgin Mary?

7/ Discuss the various heresies the characters commit against the Catholic Church and its teachings. Why does the title describe them as 'glorious'?

8/ The novel follows Ryan's coming-of-age over five years, from sensitive teenager to "a little gangster". Discuss the events that contribute to this transition and how you felt about the change in him. Could anyone have intervened to change his fate?

9/ Ryan describes his teenage love affair with Karine as something that was initially "beautiful". Do you agree? Discuss the chain of events that eats away at their relationship.

10/ Tony physically abuses Ryan and contributes to his prison sentence when he admits to a court that he has no control over his son. Does he display any saving graces as a father? Do you think his actions are genuinely motivated by a desire to protect his family?

11/ While Ryan expresses disapproval at Georgie's profession, he is partly responsible for it as he feeds her drug habit. Do either of them have alternative lifestyle choices?

12/ Georgie surmises that the perverse sexual tastes of her customers are fuelled by the ubiquitous presence of sexual images in society and the prevalence of internet porn: "what was once titillating was now everyday". Do you believe that the prevalence of sexual imagery in our society has changed attitudes and expectations towards sex?

13/ In the chapter 'What Tara Did', we finally learn the truth about the encounter between Tara and Ryan. In what way do you think it would have changed the course of events if Ryan had remembered the details of this incident? Is Tara the real villain of the novel?

14/ Many of the characters feel ashamed of their actions and seek some form of redemption. Do any of them find it? How much faith do you have in Maureen's promise to put Ryan right?

15/ Ryan observes that, "People are comfortable with stereotypes". What does he mean by this and do you agree with him? In what ways does this novel challenge working-class stereotypes?

FURTHER READING

The Green Road, Anne Enright
The Spinning Heart, Donal Ryan
City of Bohane, Kevin Barry
The Secret Scripture, Sebastian Barry
Nine Folds Make a Paper Swan, Ruth Gilligan

COMPARE & CONTRAST TO

The Goldfinch – how does Ryan's coming-of-age compare to that of Theo Decker?

The Goldfinch
by Donna Tartt

FIRST PUBLISHED

2013

LENGTH

880 pages

SETTING

New York, Las Vegas and Amsterdam

ABOUT THE BOOK

The Goldfinch begins as twenty-seven-year-old Theo Decker hides out in an Amsterdam hotel room, scanning the newspapers each day for reports of a crime he has committed. Tartt's narrative then casts back to the fateful moment, fourteen years earlier, when Theo's life derailed ... Visiting the Metropolitan Museum of Art in New York with his mother, thirteen-year-old Theo lingers in a gallery to try to speak to an enigmatic red-haired girl. At that moment, an explosion tears through the building. Theo's mother is killed but Theo survives the blast and, as he picks his way over the bodies, a dying man urges him to rescue 'The Goldfinch' - one of the priceless paintings in the gallery. The rest of the novel follows Theo's struggle to find where he belongs in a world that seems to have no place for him. As he becomes increasingly cynical and disillusioned, his lifestyle becomes more dissolute and he drifts from New York to Las Vegas to Amsterdam. At the centre of his world are two obsessions: Pippa (the red-haired girl from the gallery) and 'The Goldfinch'. It is Theo's decision to secretly hoard the priceless painting that he rescued years before that finally leads him to the crime he commits in Amsterdam.

The release of *The Goldfinch* was eagerly anticipated by devoted fans of Donna Tartt's previous work, *The Secret History* and *The Little Friend*. The ten-year wait was universally agreed to be worth it. As Stephen King neatly summarised, *The Goldfinch* is, "A smartly written literary novel that connects with the heart as well as the mind." Theo's painful journey of self-discovery is heart-breaking but also often very funny. Even the most minor characters leap off the page, while some of the major ones, such as Boris, Theo's amoral but wonderfully charismatic friend, are unforgettable.

A coming-of-age story combined with a compelling thriller, *The Goldfinch* is a modern classic. Like the painting the title refers to, this novel will endure the test of time and bring pleasure to readers for many years to come. Although the setting is contemporary, the story feels timeless, with more than a nod to Charles Dickens's *Great Expectations*. For book group discussion, this novel raises some weighty philosophical questions. Can immoral actions be justified if they lead to positive results? What makes us fall in love with certain objects and people? Can we trust our hearts to lead us to happiness? And how do we lead fruitful lives in the face of impending death?

ABOUT THE AUTHOR

Born in 1963, Donna Tartt is an American writer who grew up in Missouri. She now divides her time between the Virginia countryside and Manhattan. A very private person, she has a reputation for being enigmatic, sparked by her dislike of the trappings of literary celebrity.

Tartt's writing career has proved that dislike of the limelight is not necessarily a barrier to literary success. The publication of her debut novel, *The Secret History*, in 1992 met with immediate success and literary acclaim. A sophisticated psychological thriller, it follows the lives of a group of Classics scholars at a college in New England whose intellectual curiosity leads them to commit murder. Tartt began the novel when she was a student herself and completed it nine years later. It sold over 5 million copies and was translated into twenty four different languages.

Tartt took roughly another decade to write her following novel, *The Little Friend*. A coming-of-age novel set in 1970s Mississippi, it follows the story of Harriet, a 12-year-old girl determined to take revenge for the death of her brother. Due to the overwhelming success of *The Secret History* and the intervening gap between novels, the publication of *The Little Friend* was much anticipated. Although it was shortlisted for the Orange Prize, it failed to achieve the mass popularity of *The Secret History*. *The Goldfinch* was published in 2013. The novel met with universal acclaim from critics, became an international bestseller and won the Pulitzer Prize for fiction.

IN A NUTSHELL

A Dickensian-style literary thriller destined to become a modern classic

THEMES

Loss; love; mortality; the power of art; the random nature of fate

DISCUSSION QUESTIONS

1/ Discuss how Tartt manages to create a timeless feel in the novel. Is the Dickensian tone at odds with the contemporary setting?

2/ Theo believes that it is his mother's death that catapults his life into disaster. There are signs, however, that he was going off the rails even before this point. Does Theo have a fatal character flaw? If so, what is it?

3/ Theo's decision to walk out of the museum with 'The Goldfinch' is an impulsive action rather than a considered theft. Once he makes up his mind to keep the painting, however, he becomes culpable. How do we judge Theo over this? Does the recovery of the other artworks at the end of the novel justify his actions?

4/ Discuss the different things 'The Goldfinch' represents to Theo and why he finds himself unable to give it up.

5/ Theo and Welty share a moment of spiritual connection in Welty's dying moments. What is it that they recognise in one another? Why do you think Welty gives Theo his ring and tells him to take 'The Goldfinch'?

6/ Theo's sense of rootlessness is reflected in the different geographical locations he moves to. Discuss how Theo perceives each location (New York, Las Vegas and Amsterdam.) In what way does his perception of place mirror his own state of mind?

7/ Boris is wonderfully charismatic but he is also a bad influence on Theo. Does he enrich Theo's life or ruin it?

8/ Theo's love for Pippa is inextricably linked to the loss of his mother. Discuss what Pippa signifies to Theo and whether he ever sees her for who she truly is.

9/ Of all the characters in the novel, Mr and Mrs Barbour undergo the most startling character developments. Discuss how they change and why.

10/ Theo's major motivation in becoming engaged to Kitsey is to please Mrs Barbour. Why do you think this is so important to Theo?

11/ Is Theo justified in feeling betrayed by Kitsey's affair with Tom Cable?

12/ An ongoing debate within the novel concerns whether it is better to follow your heart or your head. Discuss the different life choices the characters make in relation to this question. Does following your heart ensure happiness? Do you think Theo should marry Kitsey or continue to pursue Pippa?

13/ One of Theo's greatest fears is that he will turn into his father. Discuss the similarities between them and any differences.

14/ The Amsterdam section of the novel involving gangsters, double-dealing and shoot-outs, is very different in plot and pace from the previous parts. Did this shift in pace and mood work?

15/ Re-read the final few passages of the novel. How did they make you feel? Did you find the ending satisfying?

FURTHER READING

The Secret History, Donna Tartt
The Improbability of Love, Hannah Rothschild
The Muse, Jessie Burton
Great Expectations, Charles Dickens
Jack Maggs, Peter Carey

COMPARE & CONTRAST TO

The Glorious Heresies - how does Theo's coming-of-age compare to that of Ryan Cusack? Also discuss the parallels between Theo's love for Pippa and Jay Gatsby's obsession with Daisy in *The Great Gatsby*.

Gone Girl
by Gillian Flynn

FIRST PUBLISHED

2012

LENGTH

463 pages

SETTING

Missouri, USA

ABOUT THE BOOK

Amy and Nick Dunne seem to be the couple who have everything. Amy is beautiful and highly-educated, while Nick is the embodiment of all-American masculinity. On their fifth wedding anniversary, however, Amy goes missing and, when traces of her blood are found at their home, Nick quickly becomes a murder suspect. His fate seems to be sealed when the police find Amy's diary, which paints a damning portrait of Nick's cruel and violent behaviour. Is it possible that Nick's protestations of innocence could be true, or is he simply a good liar? No more can be said about the plot without revealing the infamous plot twist halfway through the novel. Suffice to say, the truth about Amy and Nick's dysfunctional marriage is slowly revealed through their alternating perspectives and it isn't pretty.

While it may sound like your standard missing person thriller, *Gone Girl* has far more going for it than the average potboiler. Flynn's novel raised the bar for cliché-ridden psychological thrillers with its ingenuity, intelligence and dark humour. It is also a sharp critique of modern society, debunking the myth of the perfect marriage; highlighting the pressures on women to conform to type and raising questions about the way in which crime suspects are submitted to trial by media.

ABOUT THE AUTHOR

Gillian Flynn is an American author who lives in Chicago with her husband and son. Born in 1971, she worked as a critic for *Entertainment Weekly* before becoming a full-time novelist. *Gone Girl* was Flynn's third novel and was preceded by the psychological thrillers *Sharp Objects and Dark Places*. All three books met with commercial and critical success and their film rights were quickly snapped up. Flynn wrote the script for the movie of *Gone Girl*, starring Ben Affleck and Rosamund Pike. Critics generally agreed that the film version was just as good as the book and the movie was a huge box office success.

IN A NUTSHELL

A dark and ingenious literary thriller

THEMES

The dark side of love; deception; identity; women's gender roles; class; trial by media

DISCUSSION QUESTIONS

1/ Are there any likeable characters in *Gone Girl*? Does it matter if the characters are likeable or not?

2/ The alternating narratives of Amy and Nick highlight the different ways in which they perceive their relationship. What were their main differences in opinion? Who did you most sympathise with?

3/ Discuss how Amy and Nick's childhood experiences shape the people they become. What part does social class play in their relationship?

4/ Amy is playing 'Cool Girl' when she first meets Nick. What does this role entail? Is it true that this is the type of woman all men are looking for? Do you think, as Amy suggests, that women are guilty of colluding in the 'Cool Girl' myth? Are the pressures of doing so hard to resist?

5/ Neither Nick nor Amy can sustain the person they try to be when they first fall in love. The result for both of them is disillusionment. Discuss how their behaviour changes in the course of their relationship. Do we all adopt different personas when we fall in love? Is Amy and Nick's marriage an example (albeit an extreme one!) of the challenges that most couples in long-term relationships face?

6/ What did you make of Rand and Marybeth Elliott as characters? Is Amy's resentment towards them in any way justified? Can they really be oblivious to the fact that Amy is a monster?

7/ Discuss the portrayal of Amy and Nick's 'love' in the novel. How would you describe it? How does it relate to the novel's epigraph?

8/ Was the major plot twist a complete surprise to you?

9/ While Amy is undoubtedly mentally unstable, some of her insights into the way the world works are extremely perceptive. Did any of her observations strike a chord with you?

10/ Amy declares that she designed 'Diary Amy' to be likeable. Did she succeed?

11/ How did you feel about Amy's persecution of Nick? Did you want him to be exonerated or did you feel he deserved to be punished?

12/ How did you feel about the character of Margo? Do you think her relationship with Nick is an altogether healthy one?

13/ Female villains are relatively rare in fiction. Discuss what you found to be the most shocking aspects of Amy's behaviour. Would these characteristics have had the same impact if they belonged to a male character?

14/ Tanner Bolt claims that, thanks to Facebook, the internet and YouTube, it is impossible to achieve an unbiased jury these days. Discuss the role of trial by media in the novel. Can you think of a case where you made a snap decision about someone's guilt simply from seeing them on TV? Would you have believed Nick was guilty from his portrayal in the media?

15/ Did you find the ending satisfying? Does Amy really have the last word? How do you foresee the future for Nick and Amy after the novel has ended? What kind of parents will they make?

FURTHER READING

Dark Places, Gillian Flynn
The Silent Wife, A.S.A. Harrison
The Sudden Departure of the Frasers, Louise Candlish
Alys Always, Harriet Lane
The Woman Upstairs, Claire Messud

COMPARE & CONTRAST TO

The Girl on the Train for its shocking plot twist and portrayal of a dysfunctional marriage

The Great Gatsby
by F. Scott Fitzgerald

FIRST PUBLISHED

1925

LENGTH

172 pages

SETTING

1922, USA

ABOUT THE BOOK

In the summer of 1922, twenty-nine-year-old Nick Carraway moves to New York's Long Island after serving in World War I. Here, he is surrounded by dazzling wealth: the old established money of his cousin Daisy Buchanan and her husband, and the flashy new money of his neighbour Jay Gatsby. Nick becomes involved in both glittering worlds, visiting the Buchanans, dating Daisy's friend, Jordan, and attending Gatsby's legendary parties. As the heat of the summer builds to an unbearable intensity, however, the decadent behaviour of Nick's neighbours spirals out of control – with deadly consequences.

Like many great American novels, *The Great Gatsby* explores the theme of the American dream. It is the most celebrated literary depiction of 'the Jazz Age' – the wild decade of parties and extravagant living following World War I. Fitzgerald portrays this glamorous era as a period of moral decay where the original wholesome values of the American dream have been grotesquely distorted by greed and the empty pursuit of pleasure. Part of the genius of the way this story is told is the ambivalence of its narrator, Nick, towards the world that he is describing. Whilst he recognises that its glitz is superficial, he is also seduced by it. Readers cannot help but share this ambivalence as we are swept along with Nick's breathless descriptions of this glittering yet vacuous world.

The Great Gatsby is a must read for book groups. One of the most serious contenders for *the* 'Great American Novel,' it is consistently and deservedly ranked among the greatest works of American literature. Although it very much captures the age in which it was written, its themes are timeless and the beauty of Fitzgerald's prose is a pleasure not to be missed.

ABOUT THE AUTHOR

The American author, F. Scott Fitzgerald led a glamorous but troubled life. It is generally agreed that *The Great Gatsby* was inspired by his relationship with his wife, Zelda.

Born in 1896, he studied at Princeton University, but dropped out and enlisted in the army towards the end of World War I. In 1917, when he was stationed in Alabama, he met and fell in love with the Southern belle, Zelda Sayre. As Fitzgerald did not have the means to keep Zelda in the luxurious lifestyle she was used to, he determined he would win her by becoming a celebrated writer. When his first novel, *This Side of Paradise* was published in 1920, its success made the author a literary celebrity. He and Zelda were married and lived a hedonistic life of partying and excess which was often way beyond Fitzgerald's means. For a time, the couple moved to France where Fitzgerald made friends with celebrated writers Ernest Hemingway and Gertrude Stein, becoming part of the artistic group known as the 'Lost Generation.'

The Fitzgeralds' marriage was turbulent and largely unhappy. In 1930, after a nervous breakdown, Zelda was hospitalised and diagnosed with schizophrenia. From then on, she spent much of her life in sanatoriums. In 1937, Fitzgerald moved to Hollywood to eke out a living writing second-rate screenplays. At the age of 44, prolonged alcohol abuse took its final toll and Fitzgerald died of a heart attack. Zelda did not attend her husband's funeral and died eight years later in a hospital fire.

During his lifetime, Fitzgerald wrote a number of short story collections inspired by the Jazz Age, the most notable of which is *Tales of the Jazz Age* (1922). His other novels were *This Side of Paradise* (1920), *The Beautiful and the Damned* (1922), *Tender is the Night* (1934), *The Last Tycoon* (1941).

DISCUSSION QUESTIONS

1/ F. Scott Fitzgerald is the most famous chronicler of the Jazz Age. What do we learn about the era from *The Great Gatsby*? How do you think the author feels about it? Is it a historical period that you would have liked to experience?

2/ Fitzgerald blamed poor sales of *The Great Gatsby* on the fact that women were the main readers of novels and *Gatsby* did not contain an admirable female character. Do you think this assessment of the women in the novel is accurate? Are the male characters any more likeable than the women?

3/ What do the different geographical settings (East Egg, West Egg and the Valley of Ashes) represent in the novel?

4/ Cars, road accidents and bad driving in general are a recurring theme in the novel. What is Fitzgerald trying to say here?

5/ Is Nick's moral standpoint in the novel consistent or does he seem divided in his reactions to the other characters and their lifestyles?

6/ What information did you piece together about Jay Gatsby's past? Is he really 'Great' or is the title of the novel ironic? How did you feel about his death?

7/ How does the novel explore the theme of the American dream? What is Fitzgerald trying to say about the condition of theAmerican dream in the 1920s?

8/ Gatsby is fixated upon the Green Light he can see from his gardens. What does it represent?

9/ What do the eyes of Doctor T.J. Eckleberg symbolise?

10/ How does the description of weather conditions in the novel intensify the drama?

11/ How much can we rely on Nick's narration of events as an entirely unbiased and true one? What is the significance of the incident where Nick erases the graffiti on Gatsby's white steps before he leaves West Egg?

12/ What do you think attracts Nick to Jordan Baker? Is he gay or just scared of intimacy?

13/ Why does Daisy choose the philandering Tom over Gatsby? If Daisy had left Tom for Gatsby, would they have lived happily ever after?

14/ "Gatsby believed in the green light, the orgastic future that year by year recedes before us. It eluded us then, but that's no matter – tomorrow we will run faster, stretch out our arms further … And one fine morning -" These are the most famous lines from the novel and were engraved on Fitzgerald's headstone. What do they mean, and did you find this a satisfying ending to the book?

15/ Two very famous film adaptations have been made of *The Great Gatsby*: the 1974 version starring Robert Redford and the more recent movie featuring Leonardo DiCaprio. Have you seen either of these adaptions and, if so, how do they compare to the original novel? Would it be possible to make a film that did justice to the original text?

FURTHER READING

Tales of the Jazz Age, F. Scott Fitzgerald
The House of Mirth, Edith Wharton
Fear and Loathing in Las Vegas, Hunter S. Thompson
American Pastoral, Philip Roth
The Other Typist, Suzanne Rindell

COMPARE & CONTRAST TO

The Paying Guests for its portrayal of the 1920s or *We Were Liars* for its critique of wealth without moral responsibility

The Guernsey Literary and Potato Peel Pie Society
by Mary Ann Shaffer & Annie Barrows

FIRST PUBLISHED

2008

LENGTH

240 pages

SETTING

Post-WWII Guernsey and London

ABOUT THE BOOK

In post-war London, 1946, Juliet Ashton receives a welcome interruption to her writer's block in the form of an unexpected letter. The letter is from Dawsey Adams, a pig farmer from Guernsey, who has come upon Juliet's address in a second-hand book she once owned. Juliet learns that Mr Adams shares her admiration for the book's author, Charles Lamb, and her curiosity is sparked when he mentions that he is a member of the Guernsey Literary and Potato Peel Pie Society. This marks the start of a rewarding correspondence between Juliet, Dawsey Adams and several other members of the intriguing Society. The letters that Juliet receives are a mixture of the humorous and poignant, explaining the origins of the eccentric literary society and relating the correspondents' experiences of the German occupation of Guernsey. Inspired to write a book about her new pen friends, Juliet decides to visit the island and undertake more research. In doing so, she turns her back on the glamorous lifestyle her rich suitor, Mark Reynolds, offers to embark on a life-changing personal journey.

The Guernsey Literary and Potato Peel Pie Society provides a fascinating insight into a little-known subject: the German occupation of the Channel Islands during World War II. Shaffer slips the results of her historical research seamlessly into her narrative, detailing the impact of occupation on the islanders, from the evacuation of their children, to heroic acts of resistance, enemy collaboration and the inevitable romances with German soldiers. She also sensitively recounts the fate of the thousands of slave workers brought to the Channel Islands under Himmler's 'Death by Exhaustion' policy. At no point does the novel feel like a history lesson but by its end many readers will have learned a great deal.

This novel is also about the shared joy of reading. Almost every friendship in the story has its basis in books. Relative strangers when they first begin to meet, the members of the Guernsey Literary Society discover that literature has the power to enrich their lives and unite them as human beings. It is hard to imagine a novel more thematically suited for a book group discussion.

Mary Ann Shaffer's wit and delight in portraying the idiosyncrasies of human character are reminiscent of Jane Austen. She is also a brilliant evoker of period, capturing the feel and language of the 1940s and conveying a sense of nostalgia for an age where friends took the time to write each other letters. Perhaps most impressively, the author manages to balance the light and dark aspects of the novel, blending warmth and laugh-out-loud humour with poignancy and sorrow. The result is an ultimately uplifting novel about love, friendship and the resilience of the human spirit which makes its readers determined, at least for a while, to behave more generously towards their own friends and neighbours.

ABOUT THE AUTHORS

Mary Ann Shaffer

Many readers will be surprised to learn that Mary Ann Shaffer was in her seventies when she wrote her only published novel. Born in 1934 in Martinsburg, West Virginia, her career choices always centred around her love of books: librarianship, bookselling and editorial work. She also wrote for most of her life but never completed anything that she thought worthy of publication. Finally, with the encouragement of her book club, she embarked on *The Guernsey Literary and Potato Peel Pie Society*. The publishers she approached were immediately interested in her novel but Mary Ann fell seriously ill at this critical stage. Knowing that she did not have the stamina to complete the novel and the editorial changes required, she enlisted the help of her niece, Annie Barrows. Sadly, Mary Ann died in February 2008, prior to the publication of her novel. By this time, however, she knew that her work was to be published in at least thirteen countries.

Annie Barrows

Mary Ann's niece was eminently well-qualified to help her aunt complete the novel. Inheriting her aunt's love of books, she had also worked as a librarian, bookseller and editor and was the author of the successful *Ivy and Bean* series of books for children. Initially daunted by the prospect of completing her aunt's work, she realised that, as she had grown up listening to Mary Ann's distinctive storytelling voice, it was not as difficult as she feared to anticipate how her aunt would have completed it.

IN A NUTSHELL

A heart-warming tale of resilience and love

THEMES

War; love and friendship; the power of literature; suffering, and the resilience of the human spirit

DISCUSSION QUESTIONS

1/ One of Mary Ann Shaffer's great strengths as a writer is her portrayal of a rich variety of characters. Who was your favourite and why?

2/ Some critics have described the novel's characters as colourful to the point of caricature. Is there any truth in this criticism?

3/ *The Guernsey Literary and Potato Peel Pie Society* is as much a book about the power of literature as it is about war. What does reading do for the characters and does it hold the same power for you?

4/ What do the characters' literary preferences say about their personalities? What appeals to Isola about the Brontë sisters and why do Juliet, Dawsey and Christian share a love of Charles Lamb?

5/ What does the Literary Society offer to its members? Does your own book club provide the same things for you?

6/ Does the epistolary format of the novel make it an easy read? What are the advantages of this format? Are there any limitations?

7/ Humour plays an important role in the novel. How do Juliet and the members of the Society use humour during the war? What were your favourite comic parts of the novel?

8/ Some readers have suggested that the novel is too light-hearted to address the subject matter of war. What is your perspective? Is it possible for a 'feel good' novel to tackle war?

9/ The novel is split into two distinct parts - Juliet's letters to and from the islanders and Juliet's experience on Guernsey. Which did you prefer and why?

10/ A disproportionate number of the characters in the novel are orphans. Why do you think this is?

11/ What do Juliet and Kit gain from each other? What is the significance of Kit showing Juliet the contents of her treasure box?

12/ Did you feel the novel evoked a powerful sense of place in its depiction of Guernsey? If you have visited Guernsey, were the descriptions accurate? If you haven't, did it make you want to visit?

13/ How are London and Guernsey contrasted in the novel? What do they stand for?

14/ Did Sidney's revelation that he is gay shock you? Did you believe that he was in love with Juliet, and if so, were you hoping they would get together?

15 / Is Dawsey your idea of a romantic hero? Did your opinion of him change as the novel progressed?

FURTHER READING

Letters from Skye, Jessica Brockmole
Major Pettigrew's Last Stand, Helen Simonson
The Readers of Broken Wheel Recommend, Katarina Bivald
Hotel on the Corner of Bitter Sweet, Jamie Ford
84 Charing Cross Road, Helen Hanff
Island Madness, Tim Binding

COMPARE & CONTRAST TO

The Collected Works of A.J. Fikry for its celebration of the power of literature and *All the Light We Cannot See* for its portrayal of the resistance of ordinary people during World War II

The Heart Goes Last
by Margaret Atwood

FIRST PUBLISHED

2015

LENGTH

432 pages

SETTING

The USA in the near-future

ABOUT THE BOOK

Originally written as an online serial, *The Heart Goes Last* evolved into Margaret Atwood's fifteenth published novel. The novel is set in the USA, where a country-wide economic crash has hit north-eastern regions particularly hard. At the beginning of the novel, Stan and Charmaine, an average married couple, have lost their jobs and home. Reduced to living in their car, they are constantly in fear of being attacked by the gangs who roam the area. Little wonder, then, that the couple are seduced by an advert for the Positron project: a scheme which offers a comfortable home and job security in the town of Consilience. In exchange, the participants have to live within the privately-funded Positron prison every alternate month. Stan and Charmaine sign up for the project and, although the scheme delivers all the comforts that were promised, things soon start to go wrong. Charmaine and Stan's marriage comes under threat when they both become sexually obsessed with the 'Alternates' who live in their home while they are in prison. It also becomes increasingly clear that the price of a comfortable lifestyle is the violation of human rights and the erasure of freewill. As the couple discover the dark secrets that lie behind the project, the pressures upon their relationship intensify until Charmaine is forced to make an unthinkable choice.

Atwood lets her imagination run wild in this cautionary tale speculating on what the near-future might hold for us. At the heart of the novel is the author's interest in what happens when technology and the flaws of human nature come together. In exploring this idea, she raises many other fascinating questions about modern society and the ways we live. Would most of us sacrifice freewill in exchange for safety and security? Will technology de-personalise human relationships altogether? Could our desire for social order ultimately lead to social cleansing? And where will our desire for eternal youth lead? At the same time, Atwood also explores rich, universal themes such as the true nature of love, the perversity of sexual desire and the boundaries of identity.

ABOUT THE AUTHOR

Margaret Atwood is a Canadian novelist. She was born in Ottawa, Ontario, in 1939 and, as the daughter of a forest entomologist, spent the early years of her life living in the wilds of North Quebec. After taking her undergraduate degree at the University of Toronto, Atwood gained a master's degree from Radcliffe College, Massachusetts. She went on to teach English and then held a variety of academic posts, while writing. As well as being made a Fellow of the Royal Society of Canada, Atwood has been awarded sixteen honorary degrees; the Order of Ontario; the Norwegian Order of Literary Merit; and the Booker Prize. Throughout her life, she has been a vocal campaigner for human rights and environmental causes. She has also been notable for enthusiastically embracing new technologies in writing when many established authors have been wary or hostile towards them. A regular contributor to Twitter, Atwood has used digital fiction platforms to launch her work and helped to develop the LongPen: a digital tool enabling authors to sign books for readers on the other side of the world.

Over the years, Atwood has taken evident pleasure in experimenting with different genres and subject matter within her fiction. She is also admired as a feminist writer, creating strong, complex female characters and exploring gender ideology and sexual politics. To date she has published fifteen full-length novels, including *The Edible Woman, The Handmaid's Tale, Cat's Eye, The*

Robber Bride, Alias Grace, The Blind Assassin (winner of the Booker Prize for Fiction in 2000) and the MaddAddam trilogy (*Oryx and Crake, The Year of the Flood* and *MaddAddam*.

While Atwood is best-known for her novels, her literary output in other areas has been extraordinary. She has written short stories; screenplays; radio plays; critical articles; reviews; children's books and a number of acclaimed collections of poetry.

IN A NUTSHELL

A madcap dystopian romp exploring the disturbing avenues that human desires may take when combined with technological progress

THEMES

Utopias and dystopias; technology and 'progress'; sex and desire; the nature of love; identity

DISCUSSION QUESTIONS

1/ Atwood presents the reader with a 'warts-and-all' portrait of both Stan and Charmaine. What are their major weaknesses? Do their character flaws make them difficult to like? Did your opinion of them change as the story progressed?

2/ The author uses a third person narrative which switches between Stan and Charmaine's viewpoint. What does the dual perspective add to the story? Why do you think Atwood chose to describe events through a third person rather than a first person narrative? What is the overall tone of the narrative?

3/ Other than the material comforts it brings, are there any positive aspects to the Positron/Consilience project? What are its negatives? Does the Positron scheme have any parallels with our own crime and punishment systems? Which, if any, of the scenarios in *The Heart Goes Last* could you imagine happening in the near-future?

4/ Were you surprised when Stan's fantasy woman, Jasmine,

turned out to be Charmaine? Why does Charmaine become a "different person" with Max?

5/ Atwood only hints at the abuse Charmaine suffered as a child. How does it reveal itself in aspects of Charmaine's behaviour?

6/ Blue teddy bears appear repeatedly throughout the novel. What do they represent?

7/ As Chief Medications Administrator, Charmaine gives lethal injections to prisoners. How does she feel about this role? How does it fit with her view of herself as "sentimental"? Does she suffer any qualms of conscience? Could you have done the same in her position?

8/ Stan likes to slot women into pigeonholes. How do the women he encounters (particularly Charmaine, Jocelyn and Veronica) confound his expectations of them? Does he have any idea of what he really wants in a woman?

9/ Sexual desire is a major character motivation in *The Heart Goes Last* and technology has developed to satisfy a wide range of sexual urges and fetishes. Does Atwood overdo this theme or do you think, as a society, we are as sex-obsessed as the author seems to suggest?

10/ Through the creation of sex bots, Atwood shows just one aspect of the de-personalising impact of technology upon human relationships. Can you think of any other real-life examples? Do you think there is a real danger that technology could change the nature of human relationships irrevocably?

11/ Discuss the use and abuse of power by the characters in the novel. Do you think all utopian schemes are doomed to failure because of the flaws of human nature?

12/ Discuss the way in which the Ruby Slippers empire exploits the cult of youthfulness and the fear of ageing. Does the novel reflect our own attitudes towards ageing in this respect?

13/ While *The Heart Goes Last* explores many of the dystopian themes previously examined in Atwood's MaddAddam trilogy it has an increasingly slapstick feel as the story progresses. How did you feel about the comic elements of the book? Did you feel they worked or did they detract from the novels more serious messages?

14/ Although Stan is careful not to bring it up, he finds it difficult to forget that Charmaine had a torrid affair and once obeyed instructions to give him a lethal injection. Which do you think is harder for Stan to accept: Charmaine's infidelity or her willingness to kill him? Are his own misdemeanours just as serious as Charmaine's? Could a marriage survive such a double betrayal?

15/ At the end of the novel Charmaine is reluctant to believe Jocelyn's claim that she never underwent brain surgery. Why do you think this is? What do you think Charmaine will do with the gift of her freedom?

FURTHER READING

The Handmaid's Tale, Margaret Atwood
Oryx and Crake by Margaret Atwood
The Hunger Games, Suzanne Collins
Uglies, Scott Westerfield
Never Let Me Go, Kazuo Ishiguro

COMPARE & CONTRAST TO

1984 for its vision of the future – particularly the roles of technology, freewill and sex. Also discuss the similarities and differences between Charmaine and Stan's adventure and the journey taken by Beatrice and Axl in *The Buried Giant*.

The Help
by Kathryn Stockett

FIRST PUBLISHED

2009

LENGTH

451 pages

SETTING

The early 1960s, Mississippi, USA

ABOUT THE BOOK

In 1962 a would-be writer, Skeeter Phelan, returns to her hometown of Jackson, Mississippi, after graduating. As soon as she is on home ground, Skeeter is under pressure from her mother to follow the example of her old friend, Hilly Holbrook, who is now married with children and presides over the League - a club of genteel Southern ladies. Skeeter joins the League and attempts to re-establish her bond with old friends but is struck by the shabby way in which Hilly and co. treat their black 'help'. Seeing an opportunity to get herself published, Skeeter secretly begins collecting the stories of the black domestics in Jackson. Civil rights issues have reached boiling point in Mississippi, however, and Skeeter soon realises that, in pursuing the project, she not only risks social rejection but is also placing the lives of the maids in danger.

The Help is told from the perspective of three very different voices. As well as Skeeter's point-of-view we hear from Aibileen, a black maid who is the very embodiment of grace under pressure, and her friend, Minny, whose inability to kowtow to her white employers loses her job after job. Different as they are, the women are united in their aim to speak out against the boundaries which attempt to define and demean them.

Stockett's novel is a timely reminder that the persecution and exploitation of African Americans did not come to an end with the abolition of slavery. The author's portrayal of the segregated South in the early 1960s brings alive the realities of racial inequality in the not-so-distant past. The maids interviewed by Skeeter endure low pay, long hours and are often treated by their employers as less than human. Stockett highlights the hypocritical attitudes of the white Southern women who are happy to entrust a black woman with the raising of their children but do not wish to share a bathroom with them. Despite the harsh realities of the black lives in the novel, there is also hope and a great deal of humour to be found in the narratives of Aibileen and Minny. Stockett gives all the best lines to her black protagonists and it is their voices that emerge as the most vivid and engaging.

After its publication *The Help* became a publishing phenomenon, spending more than 100 weeks on *The New York Times* Bestseller List. The inevitable movie adaptation was Oscar-nominated and also a box-office success. Despite its throngs of admirers, however, Stockett's debut novel has had its detractors. A number of black literary critics have suggested that *The Help* is a 'white saviour' narrative (an accusation also levelled at *To Kill a Mockingbird*). While Stockett's primary subject matter is the lives of black women, these critics point out that the white author only offers these characters hope through the introduction of Skeeter, a white woman. Adding fuel to the race controversy surrounding the novel came a court case in which a black housekeeper, employed by the author's brother, attempted to sue Stockett for basing the character of Aibileen on her without permission. Stockett denied the allegation and the case was dismissed.

ABOUT THE AUTHOR

Kathryn Stockett was born in 1969 in Jackson, Mississippi. After graduating from the University of Alabama with a degree in English and creative writing she moved to New York City where she worked in magazine publishing and marketing for nine years. *The Help*, Stockett's first novel, was inspired by the racism she witnessed while growing up in the South and the close bond she shared with her family maid.

IN A NUTSHELL

A powerful critique of racism told with humour and compassion

THEMES

Segregation; racism; female solidarity; the civil rights movement; courage

DISCUSSION QUESTIONS

1/ The story is divided between the first-person voices of Aibileen, Minny and Skeeter. Which character's voice was your favourite and why?

2/ One of the main themes of *The Help* is the endemic racism in the American South. How does Stockett illustrate her characters' casually racist attitudes? Why do you think the author focuses particularly on the racism of white middle-class women?

3/ Compare the characters of Hilly Holbrook and Elizabeth Leefolt. Did you have any sympathy with Elizabeth or is her inability to follow her conscience inexcusable?

4/ While Aibileen and Minny are great friends they are as different as chalk and cheese. Discuss the differences in their response to the racism of their employers. Which type of response did you have the most sympathy with? How do each of them benefit from their friendship?

5/ Despite the harsh realities of their lives, there is a great deal of humour to be found in the narratives of Aibileen and Minny. What was your favourite humorous line or incident? Without these dashes of comedy would the content of their narratives be too bleak?

6/ Discuss the parallels between the way the women of the League treat their maids and their treatment of Celia Foote. How do you think you would have perceived Celia if she had moved into your neighbourhood? Are most of us guilty of some kind of prejudice?

7/ Do you believe Minny's hostility towards white people in general is justified? Does her attitude soften at all as the novel progresses?

8/ Discuss the relationship between Aibileen and Mae Mobley. How does Aibileen try to teach Mae Mobley that there is no difference between black and white people? Do you think Mae Mobley will remember these lessons into adulthood or become like the ladies of the League?

9/ Discuss the parallels between Aibileen's role in Mae Mobley's life and the part Constantine plays in Skeeter's upbringing. What do the black women provide that the girls do not receive from their own mothers? Are all the white women in the novel portrayed as lacking maternal instinct?

10/ What price does Skeeter pay for showing her sympathies with the civil rights movement? How difficult do you think it would have been for white Southerners to publicly support black rights at that time?

11/ Are Skeeter's motives for writing 'Help' entirely selfless? Do you think she fully appreciates the danger she is placing the maids in when she begins the project? How did you feel about her leaving Jackson at the end of the novel?

12/ What does Aibileen gain from writing her story? What do you think the future holds for her?

13/ Is it at all problematic that the black characters in the novel only achieve self-expression through the agency of a white character? Is *The Help* a novel about black women written for white women?

14/ Kathryn Stockett has stated that, when writing *The Help*, she was "scared ... that I was crossing a terrible line, writing in the voice of a black person." While many readers have praised the authentic ring of Minny and Aibileen's narrative voices, some critics have questioned the white author's credentials to write from a black perspective. How did you feel about it?

15/ How far has American society moved on from the Segregation portrayed in *The Help*? Are there still inequalities that need to be addressed?

FURTHER READING

To Kill a Mockingbird, Harper Lee
We Are All Welcome Here, Elizabeth Berg
The House Girl, Tara Conklin
A Thousand Never Evers, Shana Berg
Saving Ceecee Honeycutt, Beth Hoffman

COMPARE & CONTRAST TO

I Know Why the Caged Bird Sings for its portrayal of the African American experience from the 1930s-60s

The Humans
by Matt Haig

FIRST PUBLISHED

2013

LENGTH

304 pages

SETTING

Cambridge, England, Earth

ABOUT THE BOOK

Cambridge professor, Andrew Martin, has taken one giant leap for mankind. In finally cracking a mathematical conundrum known as the Riemann hypothesis, he holds the key to technological advances that will transform the lives of humans beyond their wildest dreams. Martin's great intellectual achievement, however, has not gone unnoticed. Inhabitants of a far-off planet, Vonnadoria, have been observing his progress with trepidation. Aware that humans are a violent and greedy race, the Vonnadorians are convinced that Earthlings would be sure to abuse such knowledge and power. To prevent this from happening, they discretely abduct and assassinate the Cambridge professor before he can share his discovery with the rest of the world. In his place they send the story's narrator, an alien who, like all Vonnadorians, has no name. The narrator's mission is to pass himself off as Andrew Martin for just long enough to destroy any evidence of the professor's discovery – i.e. data and any human beings who may have known about it. A reluctant emissary, the narrator is repulsed by the physical appearance of humans and confused by their illogical behaviour. His perspective begins to change, however, as he finds himself becoming increasingly attached to Andrew Martin's wife, Isobel, and her teenage son,

Gulliver. Aware that his resolve is wavering, the alien's Vonnadorian superiors urge him to kill Isobel and Gulliver, or someone else will be sent to do it for him.

The narrator's status as an alien, with little knowledge of the way life is conducted on Earth, provides a rich vein of comedy in this novel. Arriving naked in the middle of a motorway, he faces a steep learning curve when it comes to understanding human manners and customs (including the importance of wearing clothes). He also faces some challenges when it comes to blending in to family life. Doing his best to emulate human speech patterns, he takes Gulliver's lead by liberally sprinkling his conversation with swear words. Meanwhile, Isobel becomes suspicious when, for the first time in their married life, her husband helps her to load the dishwasher. The alien's understandable confusion over the contradictions in human behaviour brilliantly illustrates many of the absurdities in the way we choose to live. As well as poking fun at some of our sillier habits, Haig offers a more serious critique of humans' less desirable traits – our propensity for violence, our obsession with money, our xenophobia and our intolerance towards mental illness. At the same time, however, he celebrates those things that we have got right – our capacity for love and selflessness and our ability to create and appreciate great works of art, literature and music. If your book club is looking for an accessible, humorous and life-affirming read, then look no further than *The Humans*.

ABOUT THE AUTHOR

Matt Haig was born in Sheffield, England, in 1975. He studied English and History at Hull University and then took an MA at Leeds University. His debut novel, *The Last Family in England*, was published in 2004 and became a bestseller. The author's other novels include *The Dead Father's Club*, *The Possession of Mr Cave* and *The Radleys*, which won an ALA Alex Award. Haig has been open about his lifelong struggle with depression and his memoir/manual *Reasons to Stay Alive* is an account of the nervous breakdown he had in his mid-twenties. He has also written several children's books. He lives in Brighton with the writer Andrea Semple and they have two children.

IN A NUTSHELL

A funny and life-affirming exploration of the human condition, written from the perspective of an alien

THEMES

The redeeming power of love; family; mortality; the human condition; logic vs. emotion; the individual vs. the collective

DISCUSSION QUESTIONS

1/ *The Humans* is a relatively easy read, written in an accessible style and broken up into short chapters. Did you find Haig's writing style over-simplistic or does it hit just the right note?

2/ Matt Haig has said of *The Humans*, "I don't want to tell you it is a book that features an alien in it, because you might not like books with aliens in it, and I don't really." Were you put off by the sci-fi element of the story? Is it really a science fiction novel or would you classify it as something different?

3/ How does the title of the novel and the narrator's assumed readership affect the way we read *The Humans*? Would we all benefit by reassessing our lives from an alien's point of view?

4/ The narrator's alien perspective highlights many of the absurdities of human life. Which of his bemused observations struck you as particularly astute or funny?

5/ The alien protagonist observes that, "madness is sometimes a question of time, and sometimes of postcode." What does he mean by this? Do you agree?

6/ The Vonnadorians kill Andrew Martin because they fear that, given advanced technological resources, humans would find their planet and either "destroy or subjugate" them. Do you think these fears are well-founded?

7/ The narrator comes to appreciate the merits of humanity

through discovering Emily Dickinson's poetry; the music of Debussy and The Beach Boys; peanut butter; and the pleasure of canine company. Do you agree that these discoveries symbolise the best of what human life has to offer? Is there anything that you would add to the list?

8/ The narrator initially perceives Earth as "a place of death" and wonders how humans cope with the ever-present knowledge that their bodies will deteriorate and die. With this in mind, why does he later make the decision to surrender his immortality in order to become human?

9/ When he replaces Andrew Martin, the alien ironically turns out to be a better father and husband than his predecessor. In what areas does he improve the lives of Isobel and Gulliver? Is it feasible that they would still want him in their lives after he reveals his true identity?

10/ When the narrator arrives on Earth, he doesn't understand the concept of marriage and concludes that love sounds like a "delusion". How does his time with the Martin family transform these attitudes?

11/ After confessing to Isobel that he is an alien, the narrator regrets his actions and considers trying to persuade her that he is still her husband and has simply had a nervous breakdown. Could the novel be interpreted this way? Is it possible that it is a story of a neglectful husband who has a breakdown, believes he is an alien and, as a result, reconnects with his family?

12/ By building their civilisation upon logic and reason, the Vonnadorians have eliminated weather, war, pain and even death. Do you think, as the novel suggests, that a life lived without these adversities would be dull? If you were in the narrator's position, which world would you choose?

13/ The novel seems to suggest that, while humans are a race characterised by violence and greed, we are redeemed by our capacity for love. Do you agree?

14/ The narrator writes a 97 point list of advice for Gulliver. What did you think of his advice? Were there any points you particularly agreed or disagreed with?

15/ Point 14 on the list of advice reads, "Your life will have 25,000 days in it. Make sure you remember some of them." Which of the days of your own life will stand out as the truly memorable ones?

FURTHER READING

The Radleys, Matt Haig
The Curious Incident of the Dog in the Night-time, Mark Haddon
This Book Will Save Your Life, A.M. Homes
The Rosie Project, Graeme Simsion
Extremely Loud and Incredibly Close, Jonathan Safran Foer

COMPARE & CONTRAST TO

The Art of Racing in the Rain for its outsider's perspective on human life

The Husband's Secret
by Liane Moriarty

FIRST PUBLISHED

2013

LENGTH

448 pages

SETTING

Australia

ABOUT THE BOOK

The Husband's Secret begins with the intriguing moral dilemma of an Australian housewife. Cecilia Fitzpatrick, whose idyllic family life is the envy of many, discovers a sealed letter hidden in the attic. The letter is written by her husband, John-Paul, and addressed to her, but clearly states on the envelope it is only to be opened in the event of his death. As Cecilia ponders over her next action, we are introduced to two other women, also experiencing crises. Tess's world falls apart when she discovers that her husband and cousin have fallen in love with each other, while grandmother, Rachel Crowley, is horrified to learn her son and daughter-in-law are moving to New York, taking her beloved grandson with them. As the story progresses, interspersed with flashbacks from 1984, it becomes apparent what these three seemingly unconnected women have in common. Each one of them is in some way affected by the devastating impact of John-Paul's secret.

The Husband's Secret is much more than a tautly plotted page-turner. Once the secret the title refers to is revealed, the consequences for the characters are just as compelling as the mystery itself. At the heart of the novel's power is Moriarty's strong characterisation. She sensitively portrays the challenges we face at different stages of our lives: the self-absorption of the teenage years; the increased confidence but sexual obscurity of middle age and the physical frustrations of old age. Her characters are sympathetic but also deeply-flawed. Like the majority of us, they believe themselves to be 'good people' until the foundations of their lives are shaken and their secure sense of self is thrown into question.

The Berlin Wall is the predominant symbol in the novel used as a metaphor for the way, as humans, we construct internal barriers. The themes of sin, guilt and forgiveness are also thoroughly examined. Moriarty poses some interesting questions about what makes up an individual's identity, as the characters are forced to re-examine both their own sense of self, and the true identities of those around them. A thoughtful examination of love and personal responsibility, this novel raises some fascinating moral conundrums for reading groups.

ABOUT THE AUTHOR

Liane Moriarty is an Australian author who lives in Sydney and juggles writing and motherhood. She has written five bestselling novels for adults as well as the *Space Brigade* series for children. The scope of her novels ranges widely in subject matter from sibling rivalry (*Three Wishes*) to amnesia (*What Alice Forgot*) and obsessive stalking (*The Hypnotist's Love Story*). All of her work, however, demonstrates a fascination with characters who reach turning points in their lives and are forced to re-examine their identity. *The Husband's Secret* is her bestselling novel to date and the film rights have been purchased.

IN A NUTSHELL

A thought-provoking mystery packed with moral dilemmas

THEMES

Secrets & silences; moral responsibility; love; identity; guilt; sin & redemption; forgiveness

DISCUSSION QUESTIONS

1/ Liane Moriarty is particularly good at portraying flawed and ultimately very human characters. How does she achieve this? Who was your favourite and least favourite character and why?

2/ Does the multi-perspective format of the novel (from the viewpoints of Tess, Rachel, Cecilia and Janie) make it a satisfying read? What are the advantages of this format? Are there any limitations?

3/ Did you guess the contents of John-Paul's letter?

4/ Would you have opened the letter if you were in Cecilia's position?

5/ Most of the characters are harbouring a secret of some sort. Discuss the various secrets the characters conceal from one other. Is complete honesty between loved ones possible or even desirable?

6/ Cecilia tears up John-Paul's letter after she has read it. Why do you think she does this? Do you think she ever has any intention of exposing his secret?

7/ John-Paul appears to be a good person who commits an inexcusable act. The novel raises questions about whether one evil act defines a person for the rest of their lives. What is your opinion?

8/ The author portrays our teenage years as a period of temporary madness when we are at the mercy of hormones and wild emotions. Does this make John Paul's actions more forgivable?

9/ Is Will's infatuation with Felicity in any way excusable?

10/ Cecilia, Tess and Rachel are all motivated to a large degree by the desire to protect their children. Discuss the ways they try to do this and the life choices they make as a consequence. Are their attempts doomed to failure?

11/ The role of 'school mum' is an important one for both Cecilia and Tess. Cecilia defines herself by this ideal, perfecting it to an art form. Tess shies away from it, finding the social obligations so intimidating, she is put off having another baby. In your own experience, do women with children feel pressured by the image of the perfect 'school mum'?

12/ When Tess begins her affair with Connor Whitby, she contrasts the intense emotions and sensations she experiences with the more subtle pleasures of marriage. Discuss how marital love is portrayed in the novel. Does it stand a chance against the novelty of passion and excitement?

13/ Do you think Tess makes the right decision when she takes Will back? Is Cecilia's decision to stay with John-Paul an understandable one?

14/ In the Epilogue, we are introduced to a parallel future for some of the characters, showing how different their lives would have been if they had made slightly different choices. Do you feel that events are propelled by a series of accidents in the novel which the characters have no real control of, or do you feel they are masters of their destiny?

15/ Did you feel the overall mood of the novel was rather bleak or ultimately uplifting?

FURTHER READING

What Alice Forgot, Liane Moriarty
Every Last One, Anna Quindlen
Between a Mother and Her Child, Elizabeth Noble
Necessary Lies, Diane Chamberlain
Instructions for a Heatwave, Maggie O'Farrell

COMPARE & CONTRAST TO

Everything I Never Told You or *We Were Liars* for its exploration of family secrets and their impact

I Know Why the Caged Bird Sings
by Maya Angelou

FIRST PUBLISHED

1969

LENGTH

320 pages

SETTING

1930s-1940s USA

ABOUT THE BOOK

I Know Why the Caged Bird Sings is the first of seven volumes of autobiography written by Maya Angelou. It is also the most popular and critically acclaimed of her memoirs. First published in 1969, it is set in the 1930s and 1940s and documents Maya's coming-of-age as a black girl in the American South, confronting loneliness, racism, sexism and violence. The book reflects not only her personal story, but the collective experience of the African American community during that period in history.

Although it is an autobiography, *Caged Bird* is often compared with the novels *To Kill a Mockingbird* by Harper Lee and *Invisible Man* by Ralph Ellison. This comparison is valid, not only because of the similar themes of the books (i.e. prejudice, racism and the search for identity) but also because Angelou's memoir presents itself in a format more commonly found in fiction. Angelou ingeniously employs all the most effective techniques of fiction writing to make her memoir come alive. Maya's vernacular voice is vibrant and likeable, the dialogue is fresh and snappy and her childhood recollections of sensory experiences, such as the taste of fried catfish and the fragrance of tinned pineapple syrup, place the reader immediately in the moment.

Maya's early life involves many painful experiences, including abandonment by her parents and, most shockingly, her rape as an eight-year-old. Despite its brutal realities, the details of her life are told with a wit and wisdom which prevents the memoir from becoming unbearably harrowing. Angelou balances her subject matter beautifully, juxtaposing moments of despair with humour. Hilarious recollections such as "the incident" where Sister Monroe has to be prised off the visiting minister in church demonstrate that while Angelou has the deepest respect for her community, she is also able to laugh at its foibles. The tone of *Caged Bird* and its title, taken from a poem by African American poet, Paul Laurence Dunbar, clearly convey Angelou's message. In spite of the racism and oppression that the black community are confronted with, their courage and capacity for joy will not be eroded. Angelou's memoir is both a damning depiction of racism in its many forms and a joyful celebration of the black community's strength.

ABOUT THE AUTHOR

I Know Why the Caged Bird Sings covers only the first sixteen years of Maya Angelou's extraordinary life. It took six further volumes of autobiography for Angelou to adequately cover the rest. During her lifetime she also wrote non-fiction and poetry.

Born Marguerite Ann Johnson on 4th April 1928 in St. Louis, she became 'Maya' thanks to her brother's insistence on calling her "Mya Sister." When she was three years old, her parents divorced and she and Bailey were sent to live in the rural Southern town of Stamps, Arkansas with their paternal grandmother. They continued to be moved around for the rest of her childhood, from St. Louis, back to Stamps, then California and finally San Francisco. At the age of eight she was raped by her mother's boyfriend. A high achiever academically, she excelled in literature and drama and won a scholarship to study dance and drama at San Francisco's Labor School. At 14, she took time out of her studies to become the first African American streetcar conductor in San Francisco. At sixteen she became pregnant and gave birth to her son shortly after graduating.

Maya struggled to support herself and her son, taking a variety of jobs including waitressing and briefly even resorting to prostitution. She yearned for a career in the entertainment business and in 1954 she left her son in the care of her mother while she toured Europe for a year with a production of the opera, *Porgy and Bess*. At this point she also officially changed her name to Maya Angelou. She went on to study modern dance with Martha Graham and in 1957 recorded an album, 'Calypso Lady.'

In the late 1950s, Angelou moved to New York and joined the Harlem Writers' Guild where she met a number of influential African American authors including James Baldwin who became a close friend. She also joined the Civil Rights Movement after being influenced by the speeches of Civil Rights Leader, Martin Luther King Jr.

In 1960, she moved to Cairo, Egypt where she was briefly married to a South African freedom fighter. The following year she moved to Ghana, where she met Civil Rights campaigner Malcolm X and agreed to help him build his new Organisation of African American Unity. Shortly after her return to the United States in 1965, however, Malcolm X was assassinated. In 1968, Martin Luther King Jr. asked her to organise a Civil Rights march, but he too was murdered. The deaths of the two prominent Civil Rights Leaders had a profound effect on her. With the support of James Baldwin, Angelou began work on *I Know Why the Caged Bird Sings* which was published in 1969 to international acclaim.

Maya Angelou continued her work as a Civil Rights activist throughout her life. Her strong voice and intelligence were officially recognised by three Presidents of the United States. Both Gerald Ford and Jimmy Carter appointed her onto Presidential committees. In 1993, at President Bill Clinton's request, she wrote and performed a poem 'On the Pulse of Morning', for his inauguration, making her one of only two poets in American history to receive this honour. Her work in the Arts spanned literature, film and theatre. Some of her many achievements included the Presidential Medal of Arts in 2000, the Lincoln Medal in 2008, three Grammy awards, Pulitzer Prize nominations, over 50 honorary degrees and an Emmy nomination for her appearance in the television adaptation of Alex Haley's *Roots*. She also became Reynolds Professor of American studies at Wake Forest University.

Maya Angelou died on May 28th, 2014, having achieved what would seem impossible. Aware of the limitations placed upon African American women from an early age, she refused to be confined by them and proved through her achievements that prejudice has no legitimate foundations.

IN A NUTSHELL

An inspiring story of determination in the face of racism and one of the best examples of fictional autobiography

THEMES

Racism; displacement; gender; notions of beauty; family

DISCUSSION QUESTIONS

1/ What is the significance of the title, *I Know Why the Caged Bird Sings*?

2/ Discuss the opening scene of the book. Why does Angelou begin her memoir with this particular incident?

3/ Discuss Maya's relationship with Bailey. What are the similarities and differences between them? What are the things that begin to come between the siblings as they grow older?

4/ What is Maya's attitude towards religion in the novel? Does she see religious faith as helpful for the black community?

5/ Which characters serve as positive role models for Maya? What does she learn from them?

6/ Discuss the incidents of racism Maya experiences. How does she react? How do the other black characters in the novel deal with racism?

7/ Discuss Angelou's portrayal of Bailey, Big Bailey and Daddy Clidell in *Caged Bird*. What limitations do they face as black men and how do they deal with them?

8/ Angelou contrasts Momma's moral rectitude with the criminal activities of the Baxter family and Daddy Clidell's conmen friends. Both are a response to their place within a racist society. Which reaction did you have the most sympathy with and why?

9/ Angelou suggests that adolescence is particularly painful for black girls as they face the triple oppression of racism, black powerlessness and sexism. Discuss how these three factors impact on Maya.

10/ Maya and Bailey's sexuality become mixed up with their issues over parental abandonment. Discuss how this confusion presents itself.

11/ Words hold great power for Maya. Discuss this in relation to her period of muteness and her love of books.

12/ Discuss Maya's character development through the book. In what ways does she change? How does hardship shape her and make her stronger?

13/ How does *Caged Bird* compare with other autobiographies that you have read? Were there any striking differences, particularly in style and narrative voice? Did the narrative style make you feel more involved in the story or have the reverse effect?

14/ In interview, Maya Angelou admitted that she took certain liberties with the truth in her memoir (e.g. blending several characters into one to improve the characterisation). Does this bother you? Would an autobiography that didn't 'rearrange' the facts make for a boring read? Bearing in mind the subjectivity of memory, is it ever possible to produce an autobiography that is one hundred percent 'true'?

15/ In *Caged Bird*, Angelou points out the insidious way in which ideals of beauty are associated with white characteristics, e.g. as a teenager, she notes that her male counterparts are only interested in the paler-skinned black girls with straight hair. Is this still a relevant issue today?

FURTHER READING

Gather Together in my Name, Maya Angelou

Go Tell it on the Mountain, James Baldwin
The Bluest Eye, Toni Morrison
Their Eyes Were Watching God, Zora Neale Hurston
Native Son, Richard Wright

COMPARE & CONTRAST TO

The Help for its historical portrayal of the African American experience or *Americanah* to consider how far life has changed for black women in the USA

The Invention of Wings
by Sue Monk Kidd

FIRST PUBLISHED

2014

LENGTH

450 pages

SETTING

The American South in the early nineteenth century

ABOUT THE BOOK

The Invention of Wings was inspired by the true story of Sarah Grimké: one of the first female campaigners for the abolition of slavery. Presented with a ten-year-old slave girl named Hetty for her eleventh birthday, Sarah defied the conventions of Southern society and the laws of the state by becoming friends with Hetty and teaching her to read. Later, along with her sister Angelina, she became a vocal abolitionist and one of the earliest important American feminists. Despite these remarkable achievements, Sarah Grimké has been all but forgotten by history: an oversight which Monk Kidd wished to address.

The novel begins in 1803 when Hetty is first presented to Sarah. Told through the alternating perspectives of Sarah and Hetty (known as Handful) it traces the tentative friendship the girls form and their separate struggles against the restrictions imposed upon them. While Handful dreams of escaping her life as a slave, Sarah rails against the gender restrictions imposed on her and realises that she cannot live in a society that condones slavery. Spanning thirty-five years, the novel follows Sarah as she moves away from the South to begin her fight for the abolition of slavery and equal rights for women. Meanwhile, Handful plots her escape. When she learns that Handful is in danger, however, Sarah returns to the South in a bold attempt to save her.

Through the distinctive voices of Sarah and Handful, Sue Monk Kidd presents two very different personalities dealing with different, yet related, restrictions. Sarah's dawning realisation that the campaign for women's rights and the abolition of slavery are inextricably linked underlines these themes. While the novel is a worthy tribute to the remarkable Sarah Grimké, it is Handful's vibrant and defiant narrative voice that really brings the story to life.

ABOUT THE AUTHOR

Sue Monk Kidd is an American author who grew up in the South. The racial inequality she witnessed there during the fifties and sixties, including the activities of the Ku Klux Klan, led to her desire to write about racial themes. Her debut novel, *The Secret Life of Bees,* became an international bestseller and was adapted into an award-winning movie. Its successor, *The Mermaid Chair,* was also a #1 New York Times bestseller. As well as fiction, Sue Monk Kidd has written a number of acclaimed non-fiction titles including *The Dance of the Dissident Daughter*, *Where the Heart Waits* and co-authored *Travelling with Pomegranates* with her daughter Ann Kidd Taylor. She lives with her husband in Florida.

IN A NUTSHELL

A powerful portrait of American slavery drawing perceptive parallels between the restriction of the human rights of African Americans and the restrictions upon the freedom of women during this era

THEMES

Slavery; racism; gender restrictions; freedom; friendship; sisterhood; courage; faith

DISCUSSION QUESTIONS

1/ *The Invention of Wings* was inspired by the life of Sarah Grimké, an abolitionist and crusader for women's rights. In conveying Sarah Grimké's experiences, however, Sue Monk Kidd said she wanted to write a "thickly imagined story" rather than a "thinly fictionalized account". What are the advantages of fact-inspired fiction as opposed to biography? Are there any disadvantages?

2/ Did you feel the alternating narratives of Sarah and Handful were effective? Did you prefer one voice over the other?

3/ Compare the way in which Handful and Sarah are shaped by their mothers. How does this influence the women they become?

4/ Discuss the attitudes of Sarah's family towards slavery. What do they fear the consequences would be if it were abolished?

5/ Sarah and Handful's friendship is complicated by an imbalance of power. Discuss the way slavery distorts their relationship.

6/ Discuss Sarah's journey from muteness to finding her own unique voice. How is this journey reflected in her changing ambitions and her relationships with men?

7/ Discuss the importance of literacy in the novel. Why is teaching a slave to read considered such a subversive crime in the South? In what alternative ways do the illiterate characters in the novel express themselves?

8/ Discuss the different ways (both subtle and dramatic) in which the characters rebel against the restrictions of slavery.

9/ A number of the characters show great courage in the novel. Who do you think was the bravest and why?

10/ Discuss Sarah's conflicting feelings about her religious faith. What is Handful's attitude towards spirituality?

11/ What do wings come to symbolise in the novel? What are Handful and Sarah seeking freedom from? Discuss Handful's theory that, while she is a slave in body, Sarah suffers from slavery of the mind.

12/ Discuss the sense of sisterhood shared by Sarah and Handful and Sarah and Angelina. Are the relationships that women forge with each other more significant than those they form with the male characters? Are any of the male characters in the novel sympathetic?

13/ Handful's narrative paints a damning portrait of slavery. Does the fact that the novel is written by a white author make her narrative any less authentic or valid?

14/ Did you learn anything new about slavery or its abolition from the novel? Does it surprise you that Sarah Grimké's role in the abolition of slavery and the promotion of women's rights seems to have been all but forgotten?

15/ Sarah states that "the plight of the Negro will continue long after abolition", as racial prejudice will remain. How far has that prediction come true?

FURTHER READING

The Secret Life of Bees, Sue Monk Kidd
Incidents in the Life of a Slave Girl, Harriet Jacobs
Twelve Years a Slave, Solomon Northup
The Color Purple, Alice Walker
Beloved, Toni Morrison

COMPARE & CONTRAST TO

The Underground Railroad for its depiction of the horrors of slavery

Life After Life
by Kate Atkinson

FIRST PUBLISHED

2013

LENGTH

640 pages

SETTING

England, 1910-World War II

ABOUT THE BOOK

Described by Gillian Flynn as "one of the best novels I've read this century", *Life After Life* is a literary take on 'Groundhog Day'. Playing with the idea of reincarnation, Atkinson bestows her protagonist, Ursula Todd with the 'gift' of repeated lives. Unlike conventional reincarnation, however, she is destined to be born in the same place and at the same time on each occasion. Born in 1910, Ursula does not, at first, survive her birth. After several more attempts, she eventually makes it to adulthood. Steering one's destiny proves to be a tricky business, however, as Ursula finds that her own survival sometimes has unanticipated repercussions for her family and friends. Her story comes to a climax in World War II, which she experiences from both an English and a German perspective.

A hugely ambitious novel which deservedly won the Costa novel prize in 2013, *Life After Life* showcases Kate Atkinson's writing talents at their best. The author's quirky humour is nowhere better displayed than in her descriptions of the quintessentially English Todd family, who are brilliantly realised with all their flaws and idiosyncrasies. Meanwhile, later in the novel, the terrifying reality of the Blitz is brought home to the reader in all its horror.

Perhaps most impressively, however, Atkinson demonstrates in this novel that it is possible to tell the same story again and again and still create a gripping read. No matter how many lives Ursula experiences, readers cannot help but care deeply about her fate.

ABOUT THE AUTHOR

Kate Atkinson was born in 1951 in York, England. She studied English literature at the University of Dundee and went on to gain a Master's degree in 1974. After leaving University, she lived in Whitby, Yorkshire, and tried a range of jobs from legal secretarial work to teaching. On moving to Edinburgh, Scotland, she began teaching at Dundee University and wrote short stories for women's magazines, winning the 'Woman's Own' Short Story Competition in 1986. A collection of some of her best short stories was published as *Not the End of the World*.

Atkinson's debut novel, *Behind the Scenes at the Museum*, won the 1995 Whitbread Book of the Year Award. This was to be the first of many literary awards bestowed upon her work. Her services to literature were recognised when she was appointed Member of the Order of the British Empire (MBE) in 2011.

Atkinson is always surprising in her choice of subject matter and incredibly adaptable in terms of genre. While her work pushes against fixed notions of genre, her first three novels (*Behind the Scenes at the Museum*, *Human Croquet* and *Emotionally Weird*) can loosely be described as coming-of-age stories, the next four (*Case Histories; One Good Turn; When Will There be Good News?*, and *Started Early, Took My Dog*) as detective stories and the following two (*Life After Life* and *A God in Ruins*) as historical fiction. Running throughout all her fiction, however, is a very distinctive literary voice. Whatever the topic, Atkinson's work exudes a quirkiness that is entirely her own, juxta-posing the mundane with the fantastic and the comic with the darkly disturbing.

IN A NUTSHELL

A poignant and funny historical novel with a fascinating twist

THEMES

Love; loss; endurance; the horrors of war; fate; gender restrictions; the British stiff upper lip

DISCUSSION QUESTIONS

1/ Is Ursula's ability to continuously relive her life a gift, or a curse? Is it an opportunity that you would welcome?

2/ As her lives progress, Ursula is able to shape or avert certain incidents. With each 'improvement' she makes, however, she also suffers a new loss. With reference to each of her lives, discuss what Ursula gains and what she loses. Do things ever really get better for her? If you had to settle for one of Ursula's lives which one would it be and why?

3/ The structure of *Life after Life* is non-linear, circular and repetitive. Did you enjoy the novel's playful style or did you find it frustrating? How does Atkinson succeed in repeating the same events while still holding the reader's interest?

4/ The snowfall as Ursula is born and the foxes that frequent Sylvie's garden are consistent features in each of Ursula's lives. What do you think each represents? How do the frequent references to other animals (chickens, baby rabbits, wolves etc.) elaborate on the fox motif?

5/ With each incarnation, Ursula becomes more resilient. Discuss her transition from a victim of life to a proactive agent within it. What is the turning point for her?

6/ At what point does Ursula's motivation in shaping her lives become political rather than personal? Can the two agendas be separated?

7/ Despite her numerous tries at relationships with men, Ursula's only true loves are Frieda and Teddy. Is Atkinson trying to say something about the power of maternal or sibling love versus romantic love? Which of Ursula's romantic relationships do you think is the most successful? Does Ursula gain more from her romances as she becomes wiser and more experienced?

8/ How does Atkinson highlight the limited choices open to her female characters in terms of their career and marriage prospects? Does Ursula succeed in overcoming any of these limitations as her lives progress?

9/ Sylvie's character is all the more interesting for its flaws and inconsistencies. Did you sympathise with her? Do you consider her to be a good mother?

10/ In what way does Atkinson present the essence of the English character, particularly during wartime? Do you feel this is anaccurate picture of Englishness?

11/ The chapters describing the pre-war idyll of Fox Corner contrast sharply with those detailing the horrors of the Second World War. Which setting did you find most absorbing and why?

12/ In describing Ursula's work as an ARP warden, Atkinson graphically conveys the physical damage done to both buildings and human beings during World War II bombings. Was there an incident that you found particularly powerful? Did these scenes make the Blitz come alive for you?

13/ Why do you think Atkinson chose to portray one of Ursula's lives in Germany?

14/ Do you think Ursula succeeds in killing Hitler? Is this final life really her last, or do you think her lives will continue indefinitely?

15/ Ursula's ability to change certain events in her life suggests that it is possible for her to change her destiny and that of others. On the other hand, the stubborn repetition of certain elements of her life suggests the hand of fate. Is it destiny or fate that ultimately wins through? Do you believe that people have the power to change their destiny?

FURTHER READING

A God in Ruins, Kate Atkinson
Behind the Scenes at the Museum, Kate Atkinson
The Versions of Us, Laura Barnett
The Impossible Lives of Greta Wells, Andrew Sean Greer
The Time Traveler's Wife, Audrey Niffenegger

COMPARE & CONTRAST TO

The Miniaturist for its exploration of fate and destiny and *All the Light We Cannot See*/*The Guernsey Literary and Potato Peel Pie Society* for the depiction of World War II

The Light Between Oceans
by M.L. Stedman

FIRST PUBLISHED

2012

LENGTH

464 pages

SETTING

1920s Australia

ABOUT THE BOOK

M.L. Stedman's *The Light Between Oceans* is one of those rare books that succeeds in straddling the boundaries between popular and literary fiction. An international bestseller, its movie rights were immediately snapped up by DreamWorks. The novel also received literary acclaim, winning three prestigious Australian Book Industry Awards and being longlisted for the Women's Prize for Fiction.

Set in 1920s Australia, the plot centres around the lives of Tom and Isabel Sherbourne. Tom is a lighthouse keeper and the couple are the sole occupants of Janus Island, which lies 100 miles away from the Australian mainland. Although the Sherbournes love one another deeply, Isabel's sadness over her childlessness casts a shadow over their lives. One day, as Isabel tends the grave of her recently stillborn child, she hears a baby's cry. A boat has washed ashore and the Sherbournes are astonished to find it contains a dead man and a baby girl who is very much alive. Tom wants to report the incident immediately. Isabel, however, falls in love with the child and sees her arrival as a gift from God. The decision they finally make regarding the shipwrecked child has devastating consequences and raises fascinating questions about love, morality and the law.

These elements alone would be sufficient to provide all the

ingredients for a page turning novel; which *The Light Between Oceans* undoubtedly is. There is also a richness and complexity to this story which far surpasses the remit of most commercial fiction. Stedman writes beautifully. Her vivid prose captures both the beauty and the savagery of the Australian landscape. Janus Lighthouse - the striking central image of the novel - serves as a metaphor for several opposing themes: light and darkness, safety and danger, isolation and communication. The rendering of historical period in the novel is also exceptionally well-executed, conveying the collective sense of shock and loss experienced by communities following World War I.

The complexity of Stedman's characters and the enormity of the decisions that they face makes this novel an absolute gift for reading groups. Few readers will be able to complete *The Light Between Oceans* without forming strong opinions about the 'rights and wrongs' of the characters' actions and as a result, group discussion is sure to be lively.

ABOUT THE AUTHOR

M.L. Stedman was born and raised in Western Australia. Her first name is Margot, but she decided to use only her initials in her authorial name in the belief that readers do not need to know the gender of a writer to appreciate their work. Stedman worked as a lawyer in London before the publication of her first novel, *The Light Between Oceans*.

IN A NUTSHELL

A powerful historical thriller revolving around moral dilemmas and the knock-on effect of one couple's actions

THEMES

Maternal love; loss; moral responsibility; the aftermath of war; forgiveness & redemption

DISCUSSION QUESTIONS

1/ Tom is haunted by his experiences during World War I. In what way does this impact on his decisions and actions throughout the novel?

2/ Tom believes that keeping to the rules prevents men from becoming savages. Do you agree, or is Isabel right to think that love is more important than rule-following?

3/ Isabel sees the arrival of the baby on the island as a gift from God and several of the other characters try to converse with God through prayer. Discuss the role of faith in the novel.

4/ Do you think Isabel would have come to terms with her childlessness if an apparently motherless baby hadn't been thrown in her path? Does living on Janus Island intensify her craving for a child?

5/ Does Isabel have any right to think of herself as Lucy's mother?

6/ Which character's perspective did you most sympathise with and why? Did your sympathies alter as the novel progressed?

7/ The beam of Janus lighthouse illuminates the ocean for miles around, but leaves the island itself in darkness. Discuss the effects of isolation on Tom and Isabel. In what respects does it lead them into a moral darkness?

8/ Hannah has experienced a great deal more loss in her life than Isabel (her mother, her husband and her daughter). Do you think Isabel's grief for her dead babies is in any way comparable?

9/ Does Tom's love for Isabel surpass her love for him? Will the pull of maternal love always be more powerful than that of romantic love?

10/ Discuss how Frank becomes the scapegoat for the grief and loss the residents of Partaguese feel after the war. In what way does Tom also become a scapegoat for the buried emotions of the other characters?

11/ Do you think Hannah could have handled Grace's transition back into her old life better? Is she right to refuse contact between Grace and Isabel?

12/ What do you believe finally prompts Isabel's decision to confess at the police station? Did her decision surprise you?

13/ Which family do you believe Lucy-Grace should have stayed with? Can you think of any other way in which the situation could have been resolved?

14/ The redemptive power of forgiveness is an important theme in the novel. Discuss how the major characters feel about forgiveness and why.

15/ Do you think the novel implies that doing the right thing is more important than personal happiness? Is it possible to be truly happy if it is at someone else's expense?

FURTHER READING

The Island, Victoria Hislop
The Secret River, Kate Grenville
The Hand that First Held Mine, Maggie O'Farrell
The Lighthouse, Alison Moore
The Cry, Helen FitzGerald

COMPARE AND CONTRAST WITH

The Snow Child for its exploration of the pain of childlessness and maternal love, or *We Were Liars* for the impact of its island setting

The Loney
by Andrew Michael Hurley

FIRST PUBLISHED

2014

LENGTH

368 pages

SETTING

The North English coast, 1970s

ABOUT THE BOOK

In 2014 a small Yorkshire publishing house, Tartarus Press, took a chance on a work by the debut novelist Andrew Michael Hurley. Tartarus produced a limited run of 300 copies of *The Loney*: an unsettling gothic tale set on the North English coast. Despite its small beginnings, Hurley's novel became something of a literary phenomenon. Word soon spread that *The Loney* had the hallmarks of a modern classic and in 2015 the novel was reissued by the mainstream publisher, John Murray. Since then, Stephen King has hailed *The Loney* as "an amazing piece of fiction", critics have compared it to the cult film 'The Wicker Man' and the novel won the Costa First Novel Award and the British Book Awards Book of the Year 2016.

    The central focus of Hurley's story is an unnerving incident that took place in the 1970s. From the perspective of adulthood, the narrator (who remains unnamed throughout) relates the events of a childhood excursion to a bleak area of the Lancastrian coast known as 'the Loney'. The purpose of the visit is to make a pilgrimage to a Catholic shrine where the narrator's mother, Mrs Smith, hopes that her eldest son, Hanny, will be cured of his inability to speak. During their pilgrimage, however, the family encounter a sinister group of locals who hold beliefs more ancient and primitive than their own. In the strange chain of events that follow, it would appear that the Devil holds more sway in this isolated part of the world than God. As a result, the lives of the Smith family are changed forever.

Much of the power of *The Loney* lies in the eerie atmosphere Hurley creates. The stark, savage landscape of the Loney is almost a character in its own right, providing the perfect setting for the inexplicable events that take place there. Hurley's novel is, however, much more than an atmospheric horror story. Also a coming-of-age saga, the narrative follows its narrator's harsh transition from childhood innocence to an understanding of the nature of evil. Think *The Catcher in the Rye* meets Stephen King and you won't be far away from the essence of this extraordinary novel.

ABOUT THE AUTHOR

Andrew Michael Hurley is a British author who lives in Lancashire. Born in 1975, he was brought up in a Roman Catholic family. After completing an MA in Creative Writing at the Manchester Writing School, he had two collections of short stories published before settling down to write his first novel, *The Loney*.

IN A NUTSHELL

An atmospheric gothic coming-of-age tale

THEMES

Religion; the limits of faith; innocence and corruption; the nature of evil; sibling relationships; coming-of-age

DISCUSSION QUESTIONS

1/ Would you class *The Loney* as a gothic horror story or a coming-of-age tale? What elements of each genre does the novel incorporate?

2/ The geographical area known as 'the Loney' is a forbidding presence in the novel. What is it about the landscape that makes it so unsettling?

3/ Many of the author's descriptions of the natural world are stunningly beautiful. Pick out a passage that you found particularly evocative and discuss why it is so effective.

4/ Why does the author have the narrator telling the story from the perspective of middle-age? What does this add to the narrative? Why is he unnamed?

5/ Discuss the nature of the relationship between Hanny and his brother. How do their experiences at the Loney shape the adults that they become? Did their roles as adults surprise you?

6/ Mrs Smith's zealous attempts to make Hanny 'better' often border on cruelty. Is her behaviour in any way understandable? Should she just accept Hanny as he is?

7/ Father Bernard is generally popular among his new parishioners but is found wanting by Mrs Smith. What was your opinion of Father Bernard? How does his attitude to faith differ from that of Father Wilfred? Why does his presence provoke such hostility in Mrs Smith?

8/ Andrew Michael Hurley was brought up in a Catholic household. Discuss the representation of Roman Catholicism in the novel. What are the benefits of belief for the characters and what are the limitations? Would you describe *The Loney* as an anti-religious novel?

9/ The group of Catholic parishioners visit the Loney at Easter: a time in the Christian calendar strongly associated with both death and rebirth. Discuss the symbols of death and renewal used by the author in the novel. Does one take precedence over the other?

10/ Before he dies, Father Wilfred mourns the lack of religious faith in contemporary society. Do you think that organised religion is seen as increasingly irrelevant in our society? If so, what has replaced it?

11/ Andrew Michael Hurley has described his novel as "a kind of dark version of the Nativity". What was your interpretation of the strange events that lead to Hanny's cure? Who is Else? What is the significance of her baby? Are the 'miracles' that take place the work of God, the Devil, or something in between?

12/ Mrs Smith attributes Hanny's miraculous cure to God. Do you think she would still have celebrated his transformation if she suspected it was the work of the Devil?

13/ Do you think Hanny was responsible for the death of Else's baby? If not, why is he left with an overwhelming sense of guilt?

14/ Doctor Baxter believes that the narrator exhibits a "childlike worldview". What do you think he means by this? Is there any evidence to suggest that the narrator is mentally ill? How reliable is he as a narrator?

15/ Did you have trouble suspending disbelief at any point in the novel or did you find the plot entirely convincing? What was the impact of the author leaving much of the horror in his story to the reader's imagination?

FURTHER READING

The Wonder, Emma Donoghue
The Watchers, Neil Spring
Rawblood, Catriona Ward
A Head Full of Ghosts, Paul Tremblay
The Essex Serpent, Sarah Perry

COMPARE & CONTRAST TO

The Woman in Black for its conjuring of a sinister, atmospheric landscape or *The Shock of the Fall* for its exploration of childhood trauma and guilt.

A Man Called Ove
by Fredrik Backman
(translated from Swedish by Henning Koch)

FIRST PUBLISHED

2014 (UK edition)

LENGTH

294 pages

SETTING

Suburban Sweden

ABOUT THE BOOK

Originally published in Swedish, Fredrik Backman's novel started life as a blog detailing the experiences and opinions of a curmudgeonly man named Ove. It soon became clear from the blog's enthusiastic following that a full-length book would be well received and *A Man Called Ove* was born. The novel became a word-of-mouth bestseller across Europe and sold over a million copies in translation.

Although only fifty-nine years old, Ove is the very definition of a grumpy old man. Frustrated at the inability of the rest of the world to follow simple rules, he prowls his neighbourhood looking for drivers flagrantly disregarding the parking regulations. Ove's extensive list of pet hates (the Internet, self-employed people, joggers, people who can't reverse with trailers, men in white shirts, IT consultants) sums up everything that he feels is wrong with modern society.

While Ove's fixations at first seem humorously petty, Backman gradually reveals to his readers the source of each one. Ove, it turns out, has suffered a number of cruel blows in his life. Worst of all, he has lost his beloved wife Sonja and, without her, Ove decides that life is no longer worth living. His plan to kill himself proves surprisingly difficult to fulfil, however, thanks to constant intrusions from his new neighbours, a teenager who parks a bicycle in a prohibited area and a mangy cat who insists upon hanging around his garden.

Skilfully balancing pathos and humour, *A Man Called Ove* is a heart-warming story of love, loss, community and companionship. Lifting the novel above the sentimental is Backman's gentle satire on a modern society in which everything (including moral responsibility) has become disposable. While readers may not wish to completely model themselves on Ove, most will sympathise with at least some of his opinions by the end of the novel. Book club members will enjoy debating just how 'Ove' they are.

ABOUT THE AUTHOR

Fredrik Backman is a Swedish blogger, columnist and author. He lives in Stockholm with his wife and two children. His first novel, *A Man Called Ove*, was followed by *My Grandmother Sends Her Regards and Apologises* and *Britt-Marie Was Here*. Backman readily admits that he shares a number of Ove's character traits.

IN A NUTSHELL

A funny and heart-warming celebration of community spirit and old-fashioned decency

THEMES

Progress; the moral responsibility of the individual; friendship and community; ageing; love; loss

DISCUSSION QUESTIONS

1/ To what degree did you identify with Ove? What are his flaws and what are his more admirable qualities?

2/ Ove believes the world would be a better place if only everyone would be more responsible and follow the rules. Do you agree with him? Has moral responsibility become unfashionable in the modern world?

3/ Instead of using his neighbours' real names, Ove likes to identify them on his own terms (e.g. the Lanky One, the Pregnant Foreign Woman, Blonde Weed). What does this say about him? Is this a tendency that we are all, to some extent, guilty of?

4/ Backman initially portrays Ove as a stereotypical grumpy old man. How does he then get the reader to reassess this perception?

5/ Life deals Ove a number of cruel blows. Which incident from his past most surprised or shocked you? How did this episode affect his outlook on life?

6/ Ove claims that "men are what they are because of what they do. Not what they say". Discuss the ways in which he lives out this philosophy. How far do you agree with him?

7/ Ove and Sonja are completely contrasting personality types. Discuss the differences between them. What impact does Sonja have on Ove's life and what do you think attracts Sonja to Ove? In your own experience, do partnerships between opposites usually work?

8/ Rune and Ove are initially good friends. What is their friendship built upon and what comes between them?

9/ Ove is fixated with the makes and models of other people's cars. What do they signify to him?

10/ Why does Ove feel that his skills are becoming obsolete? Is there a tendency in our society to treat the elderly as if they are no longer useful?

11/ Ove plans to take his own life in a number of ways. Discuss the things that prevent him from doing so in each case. How did you feel about Backman's semi-humorous treatment of suicide?

12/ Discuss the roles of the cat, Parvaneh and Adrian in persuading Ove that life is worth living. Do you think that Parvaneh realises that Ove is planning to commit suicide? If so, what action would you have taken in her position?

13/ Ove dislikes progress of all kinds. Are there any ways in which he benefits from progress in the end?

14/ The novel skilfully balances pathos and humour. What are the funniest and the saddest parts of the novel? Which mood wins out in the end? Did the ending provide a satisfying conclusion?

15/ Backman's novel is a celebration of community spirit and the philosophy 'love thy neighbour'. In what ways do his characters live out this philosophy and in what ways do they fail? In reality, is the world mostly made up of generous-spirited Parvanehs or does most of the population consist of Blonde Weeds and men in white shirts?

FURTHER READING

The Penguin Lessons, Tom Mitchell
A Street Cat Named Bob: And How He Saved My Life, James Bowen
My Grandmother Sends Her Regards and Apologises, Fredrik Backman
The Hundred-Year-Old Man Who Climbed Out of the Window and Disappeared, Jonas Jonasson
Major Pettigrew's Last Stand, Helen Simonson

COMPARE & CONTRAST TO

The Humans for the protagonist's discovery of the joys of companionship or *The Storied Life of A.J. Fikry* for its portrayal of a man who is forced to re-engage with the world

The Miniaturist
by Jessie Burton

FIRST PUBLISHED

2014

LENGTH

400 pages

SETTING

Seventeenth century Amsterdam

ABOUT THE BOOK

While the majority of debut novelists struggle to attract a publisher, Jessie Burton found herself in the enviable position of being able to pick and choose when her first novel went out to publishers. Gripped by the novel's unusual premise, publishers embarked on a bidding war to secure the rights for *The Miniaturist*. In the end, Picador triumphed with a two-book contract reputed to be worth a six-figure sum. As predicted, the novel was a critical and commercial success, selling over a million copies worldwide and winning the Waterstones Book of the Year in 2014.

Burton's novel was inspired by a visit to the Rijksmuseum in Amsterdam where the British writer saw Petronella Oortman's cabinet house. A traditional gift for Dutch girls before marriage, cabinet houses were large-scale dolls' houses designed to educate young females in the art of keeping house. Petronella Oortman's was a particularly fine example. Costing as much as a full-size townhouse, it took nineteen years to make and contained miniature replicas of everything Petronella possessed in her real home.

The Miniaturist opens in 1687, during the golden age of the Netherlands, when Amsterdam was a city of contradictions. Although many of its inhabitants were hugely wealthy and lived in great luxury, the legacy of Calvinism meant that they felt guilty about their prosperity and feared God's retribution. Into this atmosphere of moral anxiety the author drops eighteen-year-old Nella Oortman who arrives in Amsterdam as the bride of wealthy merchant, Johannes Brandt. Nella's expectations of the intimacies of marriage are quickly dashed on entering the Brandt household. Johannes's sister, Marin, is severe and unwelcoming while Johannes actively avoids his new bride and makes no attempt to consummate the marriage. Feeling that she is trapped inside a house of secrets without the key, Nella distracts herself by employing the talents of a miniaturist to make items for the cabinet house that Johannes presented to her as a wedding gift. Nella gets more than she bargains for, however, as the mysterious miniaturist begins to send unrequested items that seem to chillingly predict future events.

A unique mix of historical novel, coming-of-age tale and literary thriller, *The Miniaturist* deserves the praise lavished upon it by eager publishing houses. While providing a fascinating insight into a particular historical period, it also raises thought-provoking questions about the nature of love, the concept of family and how much control each of us has over our fate.

ABOUT THE AUTHOR

Jessie Burton is a British author, born in London in 1982. She studied at Oxford University and the Central School of Speech and Drama and was a struggling actress before she wrote *The Miniaturist*. Her second novel, *The Muse*, was published in 2016.

IN A NUTSHELL

A compelling historical mystery

THEMES

Women's gender roles & autonomy; spirituality vs. materialism; freedom; identity; fate; love; family

DISCUSSION QUESTIONS

1/ Jessie Burton brilliantly conjures up a specific period of history without overburdening her novel with historical minutiae. How do you think she achieves this? Did you learn anything new about 'the Golden Age' of Amsterdam from this novel?

2/ Nella observes of Johannes and Marin that they seem to be "obsessed with souls and purses." How does this sum up the conflicting aspects of seventeenth century Amsterdam?

3/ To our modern sensibilities, a doll's house seems a peculiar wedding gift for a grown woman. Why does Johannes buy Nella the cabinet house? What is its purpose? How does Nella feel about it?

4/ Marin, at first, appears to be a severely austere woman. Discuss the way in which Burton gradually reveals Marin's sensual side. What was your opinion of her by the end of the novel?

5/ The bird and cage imagery in the novel reflect Nella's initial feeling that she is trapped within a household she does not understand. As time goes on, however, she comes to realise that the Brandt house offers its inhabitants an unusual amount of liberty. Discuss the ways in which the household defies convention.

6/ Although Johannes cannot offer Nella a conventional marriage he turns out to be a good husband in some respects. What are his merits as a husband? If Johannes had survived, could the marriage have worked? How does the relationship between Nella and Johannes change during the course of the novel?

7/ Ironically, Nella 'comes of age' not, as she expects, through marriage but through her association with the miniaturist and Marin. What does she learn from these two women and how does their influence change her?

8/ In seventeenth century Amsterdam female power is checked by the prohibition of women from guilds and civic positions. Discuss the ways in which women, nevertheless, are shown to exert considerable power in society, albeit from behind the scenes.

9/ Johannes's fate is inextricably linked with the sugar he stores in his warehouse. With this in mind, discuss the confectionary imagery in the novel. What does sugar represent in Amsterdam? Why do you think Johannes drags his heels in finding buyers for the sugar?

10/ Johannes is sympathetically drawn but is also shown to be the cause of the downfall of the Brandt household. How did you feel about him as a character? Should he have exercised more caution, or is he a heroic victim of circumstances?

11/ Nature Morte was a favourite subject of the great painters known as the Dutch Masters. These paintings, depicting dead game birds, fruit on the point of decay, skulls etc. were intended to be a humbling reminder of human mortality. Why do you think Nella turns the Nature Morte in her bedroom to face the wall? What other images of death and decay can be found in the novel?

12/ Nella initially assumes that the miniaturist is a man. How does it change her perspective when she discovers she is a woman? Are the subtle changes to the miniatures (the mark on Rezeki's head, Marin's pregnancy bump etc.) real, or a figment of Nella's imagination?

13/ The miniatures sent to Nella seem to suggest that the fates of those in the Brandt household have already been mapped out. On the other hand, on one of her parcels, the miniaturist writes: "EVERY WOMAN IS THE ARCHITECT OF HER OWN FORTUNE". How much control do the female characters have over their own fates? Why do you think the miniaturist chooses to send this motto to Nella?

14/ Discuss the way in which Otto and Johannes become scapegoats for the prejudices of Amsterdam society.

15/ What did you think of the ending of the novel? Were you disappointed that the author doesn't reveal more about the miniaturist? Who, or what, was the miniaturist and what were her motivations? Is it a coincidence that she shares Nella's Christian name?

FURTHER READING

The Muse, Jessie Burton
The Journal of Dora Damage, Belinda Starling
The Signature of All Things, Elizabeth Gilbert
Burial Rites, Hannah Kent
The Fair Fight, Anna Freeman

COMPARE & CONTRAST TO

Life After Life for its exploration of fate and destiny

My Brilliant Friend
by Elena Ferrante
(Translated from Italian by Ann Goldstein)

FIRST PUBLISHED

2012

LENGTH

336 pages

SETTING

1950s Naples, Italy

ABOUT THE BOOK

My Brilliant Friend is the first of a series of Italian novels known as the Neapolitan quartet. The four novels follow the lives of two friends, Elena and Lila, from their childhood in a poverty-stricken area of Naples in the 1950s to their old age. The first novel, written from Elena's perspective, tells the story of the girls from first grade to the age of sixteen. Determined to escape the fates of their downtrodden mothers, Elena and Lila plan to educate themselves to better lives. They soon discover, however, that the restrictions placed upon them by both gender roles and class may be more difficult to escape than they imagined.

When they were first translated into English the Neapolitan novels caused something of a literary sensation among critics and readers alike. Critics hailed Ferrante's writing style as unique (one compared the author to an angry Jane Austen), while readers couldn't wait for the next instalment to be published. The addictive nature of these novels has a good deal to do with the disturbing nature of the friendship between Elena and Lila. While their relationship endures the years, it is compellingly toxic and has to be one of the most brutally frank portrayals of friendship ever written. Ferrante's writing style is also strangely mesmeric, dragging the reader along with Elena's mercurial emotions as she comes of age in a violent and sexist world.

Ferrante's style is not for everyone. Readers will either fall in love with this novel or find its dark tone just too much to handle. Whatever the reaction, this novel is sure to create lively debate. Those in the know have marked it out as a future classic. Read it and see if your group agrees.

ABOUT THE AUTHOR

Elena Ferrante is the pen name of an Italian novelist whose true identity is not publicly known. Even the American Italian translator of Ferrante's novels, Ann Goldstein, claims not to know Ferrante's true identity and has stood in for the Italian author at publicity events.

Ironically, while Ferrante hoped that her anonymity would focus attention away from her and towards her books, it seems to have had the reverse effect. The mystery surrounding her identity has led to many rumours in literary circles. Could her novels be the product of a collaboration of authors? Or, most contentiously, could the Italian novels that speak so eloquently of female experience have been written by a man?

While her official website reveals only that she was born in Naples, Ferrante has revealed a little more about herself in correspondence with journalists. The theory that Ferrante is a man is contradicted by her reference to herself as a mother. She has also revealed that she does not come from a wealthy background and found "climbing the economic ladder" a struggle. Other than this, she has revealed that she has a classics degree and, as well as writing, translates and teaches for a living. Ferrante's reluctance to reveal any more about herself has led critics to assume that her work is largely autobiographical. Much has been made of her decision to give the narrator of her Neapolitan novels the name Elena and several of her novels address the conflicting demands of being a writer and a mother.

IN A NUTSHELL

An explosive coming-of-age tale

THEMES

The novel examines some meaty themes including friendship; rivalry; sexuality; women & gender roles; class, and the art of writing.

DISCUSSION QUESTIONS

1/ Discuss the opposing characteristics of Elena and Lila. Which character did you most sympathise with?

2/ The moment when Lila drops Elena's doll into the cellar is crucial in the development of their friendship. How does this moment sum up the future dynamics of their relationship? Do you think the girls' treatment of their dolls has any other significance?

3/ Discuss Ferrante's unsentimental portrait of female friendship. How does it differ from other novels about friendship that you have read? Is the friendship Elena and Lila share normal or dysfunctional? Do you think Elena's decision to tell Lila's story is an act of love or revenge?

4/ The incident where Elena and Lila unsuccessfully attempt to walk to the sea highlights surprising character traits in both girls. What does it tell us about Elena and Lila? Do you think Elena might be right in suspecting ulterior motives for the escapade on Lila's part?

5/ Ferrante portrays Naples as a simmering cauldron of violence. What are the catalysts for this violence? How does it affect Elena, Lila and the other young people of the neighborhood?

6/ Discuss Elena's feelings about her mother. Do you think Elena is fair in her assessment of her mother? Why is she so fixated by her physical flaws?

7/ Why do you think Elena is attracted to Nino? Is he worthy of her affection?

8/ When Lila hits puberty she becomes a magnet for the young men of the neighborhood. Other than her beauty, what is it about her that attracts them? How do you think Lila feels about her sexual power?

9/ Elena describes Lila's transformation from an ugly duckling to a swan. Did you notice any other fairy tale imagery in the novel? Why do you think Ferrante draws on these images in what is essentially a realist novel?

10/ What is the role of the elementary school teacher, Maestra Oliviero, in the novel? Why does she claim not to recognise Lila when she personally delivers an invitation to her wedding?

11/ In her narrative Elena makes a clear distinction between those who speak in Neapolitan dialect and those who speak Italian. What is the significance of this distinction? How does it reflect Elena's own aspirations?

12/ Were you surprised when Elena turned out to be the 'brilliant friend' in the friendship? Do you think the title really refers to Elena or Lila?

13/ The climax of the novel comes when Marcello walks into Lila's wedding reception wearing the first pair of shoes she designed and helped to make. What is the significance of this seemingly minor incident? Why is Lila so upset? What does the incident indicate about Stefano's character?

14/ Some readers have suggested that only women can fully appreciate Elena Ferrante's novels. Do you think this is true or does she transcend the limitations of gender? Is there any possibility that the author of *My Brilliant Friend* could be a man?

15/ Fans of Ferrante have compared the addictive quality of the Neapolitan quartet to a literary soap opera. Has reading *My Brilliant Friend* inspired you to read the other Neapolitan novels?

FURTHER READING

The Story of a New Name, Elena Ferrante

Those Who Leave and Those Who Stay, Elena Ferrante
The Story of the Lost Child, Elena Ferrante
The Little Friend, Donna Tartt
My Struggle, Karl Ove Knausgaard

COMPARE & CONTRAST TO

My Name is Lucy Barton for its portrayal of childhood abuse, poverty and difficult mother/daughter relationships, or *The Girls* for its exploration of the pressure gender roles place upon developing young women

My Name is Lucy Barton
by Elizabeth Strout

FIRST PUBLISHED

2016

LENGTH

208 pages

SETTING

New York, USA

ABOUT THE BOOK

As the title of Elizabeth Strout's novel suggests, *My Name is Lucy Barton* reads very much like a memoir. With the perspective of hindsight, the eponymous protagonist describes a nine-week period in the 1980s which she spent in hospital. After having her appendix removed in a straightforward operation, Lucy falls mysteriously ill and undergoes a series of tests at the instruction of her concerned doctor. Feeling isolated and pining for her two daughters, Lucy is astonished and delighted when her estranged mother makes the long journey to visit her and stays for five days and nights. During her visit, they mainly talk about the lives of women from their hometown of Amgash, Illinois. While these conversations seem to bring mother and daughter together, they also circle around the many things that are unsayable about their family history which, Lucy slowly reveals, involves poverty, neglect and abuse.

 At first glance *My Name is Lucy Barton* might be mistaken for a small book both in size and scope. On beginning to read it, however, it quickly becomes apparent to the reader that this is an ordinary story told in an extraordinary manner. While the momentum of the novel is driven by a series of anecdotes rather than an all-consuming plot, the apparently everyday moments that

Lucy describes are charged with significance. Powerful, subtle and affecting, this slim novel expresses more about the nature of being human than many much weightier tomes.

Much of this novel's emotional power stems from its strongly autobiographical feel. Lucy's first-person voice is invitingly engaging and feels utterly authentic. Readers get to know her by piecing all her little anecdotes together, in the same way they would get to know a friend. Although damaged and vulnerable, Lucy is also surprisingly optimistic and possesses a generous heart. After finishing the novel, many readers will mourn her absence from their lives. For book groups there are also huge themes to discuss here, including the complexity of mother-daughter relationships; loneliness; social exclusion; class; the nature of love, and the purpose of fiction. For a little book about a relatively ordinary life, *My Name is Lucy Barton* packs an incredibly powerful punch.

ABOUT THE AUTHOR

Elizabeth Strout is a Pulitzer Prize-winning American novelist, short story writer and academic. Born in 1956 in Portland, Maine, she was raised by strict parents who were both academics. Following her graduation from a liberal arts college in Maine, Strout went on to law school. After practising as "an awful, awful lawyer for six months", however, Strout realised that it was not the profession for her and returned to her first love - writing. Her reputation as a writer slowly grew with the publication of a number of short stories and then her first novel, *Amy and Isabelle*, in 1998. Strout only became a household name, however, with the publication of *Olive Kitteridge* in 2008 which won the Pulitzer Prize for fiction. Strout currently lives in Manhattan.

While Strout's five published novels vary in subject matter, they have certain elements in common. Several are set in small towns in New England and explore similar themes: family dynamics; loneliness; social judgement; grief and childhood fears. As a writer, Strout is essentially interested in character and her great strength is a resistance to sentimentality. Strout's novels portray the nature of human experience in a subtle and truthful way through characters who are flawed and all the more human for it.

IN A NUTSHELL

An incredibly moving examination of child/parent relationships

THEMES

Mother/daughter relationships; childhood abuse; loneliness; poverty and class; truth in art; the nature of love

DISCUSSION QUESTIONS

1/ The novel has a strongly autobiographical feel to it. How does Strout achieve this?

2/ Lucy's story is told in a non-chronological way to reflect her train of thought. Did you find this effective? What impact does this technique have on the reader?

3/ The plot of *Lucy Barton* can be summarised in a couple of sentences. With this in mind, what is it that drives the narrative forward? How important is plot to you when you are choosing a novel? Has reading this novel made you re-evaluate your ideas about the importance of plot?

4/ Discuss the dynamic between Lucy and her mother. Did you feel any sympathy for Lucy's mother?

5/ Lucy's mother tells her daughter a number of anecdotes about old friends and neighbours from their hometown. What purpose do these stories serve? Why is Lucy particularly affected by the story of Kathie Nicely?

6/ Why is Lucy drawn to the statue of the starving man and his children in the Metropolitan Museum of Art?

7/ How would you describe the relationship between Lucy and her doctor? What does he represent to Lucy? How did you interpret the moment when he kisses his fist and holds it in the air before leaving Lucy's room?

8/ Were you surprised to discover that Lucy's first marriage didn't work out? In hindsight, what clues does Strout include to indicate that all is not well between Lucy and William? Do you think it is entirely William's fault that their relationship fails?

9/ Discuss the way the author portrays loneliness in the novel. Is New York an antidote to Lucy's loneliness?

10/ When Lucy first sees Sarah Payne she feels drawn to her. Why do you think this is? What do the two women have in common?

11/ Lucy is interested in, "how we find ways to feel superior to another person, another group of people" and believes this characteristic to be, "the lowest part of who we are". What examples of this unpleasant human trait does she give in her narrative? Do you agree that it is a common human failing?

12/ What is the role of Lucy's brother in the story? Why does he appear to be so much more damaged by his childhood than his sisters? How do the rest of the family feel about him?

13/ Discuss the relationship between Vicky and Lucy. Were you surprised that their shared experiences in childhood didn't make them closer? Why does Vicky seem so resentful of her sister? Why does Lucy feel that Vicky is entitled to all the money she sends her?

14/ Discuss the way Lucy's growing sense of herself as a writer mirrors her developing sense of herself as an individual. In what respect does Lucy exceed the achievements of her mentor, Sarah Payne?

15/ Sarah Payne claims that all writers have only "one story". What does she mean by this and do you agree with her? If you were to write a novel, what would your 'one story' be?

FURTHER READING

Olive Kitteridge, Elizabeth Strout
Left Neglected, Lisa Genova
Dept. of Speculation, Jenny Offill

Lila, Marilynne Robinson
Mrs Dalloway, Virginia Woolf

COMPARE & CONTRAST TO

My Brilliant Friend for its portrayal of childhood abuse, poverty and difficult mother/daughter relationships, or to *We Were Liars* for its exploration of family silences and repression

The Paying Guests
by Sarah Waters

FIRST PUBLISHED

2014

LENGTH

499 pages

SETTING

1920s London

ABOUT THE BOOK

In 1922, genteel Frances Wray and her widowed mother are forced to take in lodgers in order to keep their large villa just outside London. Their 'paying guests' are Lilian and Leonard Barber, a young married couple. At first, Frances finds sharing her home with these brash strangers an unsettling experience. As time goes on, however, she develops an increasing intimacy with Lilian. Little does Frances suspect that this burgeoning friendship will eventually lead to a murder being committed under her roof.

One of the sources of inspiration for *The Paying Guests* was a notorious British trial known as the Thompson-Bywaters case. In Waters' novel, however, the author reimagines the circumstances of the original crime of passion with a lesbian love story at its centre. Under the roof of the Wrays' suburban villa, sexual tensions mount along with the heat of the summer, evoking a growing certainty in the reader that things are going to end messily.

Underlying this tale of passion and crime is an incisive examination of the social and economic change taking place in Britain following World War I. While the genteel Wrays find themselves in seriously reduced circumstances, the Barbers, who would probably have worked as servants for the Wrays only a decade before, are now the ones with disposable income and growing power. The irony in the situation is beautifully captured in the discomfort Frances and her mother initially feel when their house is invaded by the Barbers and their gaudy belongings. Meanwhile, London still bears the emotional and physical scars of the war. Young men are few and far between and those who have been lucky enough to survive return to a changed world in which women seem to be enjoying new (albeit limited) freedoms. An intriguing blend of historical novel, love-story and fictionalised true-crime, *The Paying Guests* has something for everyone. While the attention to historical detail is superb, Waters never lets it get in the way of her compelling plot.

ABOUT THE AUTHOR

Sarah Waters is a British writer, born in Wales in 1966. Before becoming a novelist, she worked in academia, earning a doctorate and teaching English literature. All of Waters' novels - *Tipping the Velvet*, *Affinity*, *Fingersmith*, *The Night Watch* and *The Little Stranger* are historical, evoking an England of the past. With the exception of *The Little Stranger*, her novels also have a lesbian theme. Waters' literary awards have included the Betty Trask, the Somerset Maugham and the CWA Ellis Peters dagger. *Fingersmith*, *The Night Watch* and *The Little Stranger* were all shortlisted for the Man Booker Prize.

IN A NUTSHELL

A compelling mix of historical thriller, lesbian romance and courtroom drama

THEMES

Social change; class conflict; lesbian love; changing women's roles; the aftermath of World War I

DISCUSSION QUESTIONS

1/ Frances and Lilian are complex and sometimes selfish individuals. Do their flaws make them unsympathetic as characters?

2/ What restrictions do Lilian and Frances face as women? Which of them is more liberated?

3/ Do you think Frances and Lilian are well-suited? Are they equally invested in their relationship? Do they have a future?

4/ Did the fact that the love story in *The Paying Guests* was between two women affect the way you perceived it?

5/ Frances accuses Lilian of "taking the wall" in their relationship. Is this a fair criticism, or does Frances encourage this behaviour? Does the balance of their relationship change as the story develops?

6/ Waters uses domestic imagery to reflect the moral chaos that Frances and Lilian descend into. How does she do this?

7/ The Wrays' house is an imposing presence in the novel, almost becoming a character in its own right. How does Waters' description of the house reflect the sense of a dying age and also the emotions of those who live in it?

8/ On balance, is *The Paying Guests* more of a romance or a crime story? Which element of the story did you find most engaging?

9/ The aftermath of World War I pervades the atmosphere of *The Paying Guests*. In what ways has the war changed society generally and how has it affected individual characters in the novel?

10/ How did you feel about the character of Leonard? Why do you think Waters emphasises his vitality and the fact that he seems "untouched" by the war? Does his death have a deeper significance?

11/ As time goes on, Lilian and Frances put forward several different arguments to justify not going to the police. How did you feel about the justifications they offer? If Spencer had been found guilty, do you think they would have given themselves up?

12/ Bravery is a recurring theme in the novel. Which characters did you feel displayed the greatest bravery and why?

13/ Due to his unlikeable persona and the influence of the media, Spencer Ward is almost wrongly convicted of murder. If you had been present at Spencer's trial, would you have believed he was guilty? Are miscarriages of justice still a distinct possibility today, despite progress in forensic science?

14/ Were you surprised by the way the story ended? Would you have liked it to end differently? If so, how would you change it?

15/ Have you read any other novels by Sarah Waters? If so, how do you feel *The Paying Guests* compares?

FURTHER READING

Affinity, Sarah Waters
Fingersmith, Sarah Waters
Fred and Edie, Jill Dawson
Patience and Sarah, Isabel Miller
Why Be Happy When You Could Be Normal, Jeanette Winterson

COMPARE & CONTRAST TO

The Great Gatsby for its rendering of the 1920s, or *A Place Called Winter* for its exploration of historical attitudes towards homosexuality

A Place Called Winter
by Patrick Gale

FIRST PUBLISHED

2015

LENGTH

354 pages

SETTING

England and the Canadian prairies, the beginning of the twentieth century

ABOUT THE BOOK

Harry Cane is a wealthy Edwardian gentleman who has never had to work for a living. Although he doesn't possess the confidence of his gregarious brother, Jack, Harry seems set for a life of ease and comfort. Conveniently marrying the sister of Jack's fiancée, he relocates to the seaside with his new bride, Winnie, and they soon have a daughter. Nevertheless, Harry feels that he is living only a half-life until an encounter with a stranger wakes him from his torpor. Harry embarks on a secret life, the details of which are soon discovered by Winnie's family. Given the choice between disgrace and possible imprisonment or emigration, Harry leaves his wife and young child to start a new life as a homesteader in the Canadian prairies. Here he throws himself into the hard physical graft and, surprisingly, finds love. His newfound freedom and sense of wellbeing are threatened, however, by an unwelcome interloper who seems determined to thwart Harry's quest for happiness.

Patrick Gale was inspired to write *A Place Called Winter* by a family mystery that had intrigued him for some time. The author's great-grandfather, whose real name was Harry Cane, was a wealthy married gentleman who suddenly left his wife and daughter in

England to begin a new life as a homesteader in the Canadian prairies. The reason for his departure was never disclosed but he clearly left under a cloud and his daughter was discouraged from contacting him. In *A Place Called Winter*, Gale offers a feasible solution to the mystery (that his great-grandfather may have been homosexual).

A Place Called Winter was chosen by both BBC Radio 2 and Waterstones for their book clubs, for very good reason. Gale portrays Harry's character with great empathy and readers cannot help but sympathise with the conflict he feels between following convention or his heart. The author also powerfully conveys the oppressive nature of a society which stamps out any behaviour considered not to fit in with the norm. Gale's thorough historical research shows in his vivid descriptions of the physical hardships the first European settlers suffered in the unforgiving Canadian landscape. At the same time, the author doesn't shrink from addressing the impact of that settlement upon Native Canadians. A fine blend of pioneering story and thriller, *A Place Called Winter* is a compelling read featuring one of the most memorable literary villains of recent times.

ABOUT THE AUTHOR

Patrick Gale was born in 1962 on the Isle of Wight where his father was Prison Governor. He and his family moved, first to London, where his father ran HM Prison Wandsworth, and then to Winchester. Gale attended boarding school in Winchester and went on to read English at New College, Oxford. Never wanting to be anything other than a writer, Gale initially took on a variety of jobs (typist, singing waiter, ghost writer and increasingly book reviewer) to make ends meet while pursuing his art. After the publication of his first two novels in 1986, he moved to Cornwall. He now lives with his husband on a farm close to Land's End where they raise beef cattle and grow barley. *A Place Called Winter* is Gale's sixteenth published novel and was shortlisted for the Costa Novel Prize, the Walter Scott Prize and the 2016 Independent Booksellers' Book of the Year Award. His previous works include *Rough Music*, *A Perfectly Good Man* and, another book club favourite, *Notes from an Exhibition*.

IN A NUTSHELL

A moving account of a gay man's quest for identity in Edwardian England and the wilds of Canada

THEMES

Homosexuality; prejudice; repression vs. desire; freedom; colonialism; loneliness; love

DISCUSSION QUESTIONS

1/ At the beginning of the novel we see Harry Cane as an inmate in a hospital for the mentally ill. Why does the author choose to reveal this aspect of the plot so early on? How did the knowledge impact on your reading experience?

2/ What is it that draws Harry and Winnie together? Is their relationship completely loveless? Do you think their marriage would have lasted if Winnie's brother hadn't intervened?

3/ Given the historical context, is it plausible that Harry should only realise he is gay after he marries? Does the acknowledgement of gay culture in today's society make it easier for people to recognise their sexual orientation?

4/ "England has always been disinclined to accept human nature". What is the relevance of this E.M. Forster quotation to the themes of *A Place Called Winter*?

5/ Until they marry the Wells sisters, Harry and Jack enjoy a close and supportive fraternal relationship. Were you surprised by Jack's decision to eventually cut off contact with Harry? Is this a sign of weakness in Jack's character or a testament to the rigid conventions of Edwardian society?

6/ What was your initial opinion of Dr Gideon Ormshaw and his approach to mental health? Did your opinion of his character and professional integrity change as the novel went on?

7/ Gale describes Troels Munck as "the scariest villain I've ever written". What makes him so sinister and why is Harry drawn to him? What does Troels really want from Harry and Petra?

8/ The prairies of Canada are so vividly described that they almost become another character. How does working in this harsh landscape change Harry's character?

9/ One of the questions the novel examines is what it means to be civilised. How does the author contrast the mores of 'civilised' society with truly civilised behaviour? Who, in your opinion, are the most and the least civilised characters in the book?

10/ Set at the beginning of the twentieth century, the novel explores the possibilities of the New World on more than one level. Discuss the way the author highlights some of the changes taking place during this period (e.g. the emergence of women's rights, changes in class structure, medical and psychiatric developments).

11/ Native Canadians are a discreet yet haunting presence in the novel, from the few remaining camps of Cree who linger near Winter, to the presence of Ursula at Bethel. Why does the author choose to include them in his story?

12/ How does Harry's relationship with Ursula aid his journey to self-acceptance? What parallels exist between the two characters and how do they differ?

13/ Gale has described his novel as a blend of E.M. Forster's *Maurice* and Annie Proulx's *Brokeback Mountain*. Do you think *A Place Called Winter* is comparable to these epic gay love stories?

14/ Harry and Paul are united in their love and admiration for Petra. What influence does she have on both men? Do you think the relationship between Harry and Paul will continue to flourish in her absence?

15/ The novel is set in the shadow of the notorious trials of homosexuals in England in the 1890s. Did the story make you think more deeply about how dangerous it was to be homosexual during this era? At what point do you think attitudes to homosexuality began to change? Does 'coming out' still require courage today?

FURTHER READING

Notes from an Exhibition, Patrick Gale
Maurice, E. M. Forster
Brokeback Mountain, Annie Proulx
Days Without End, Sebastian Barry
Salt Creek, Lucy Treloar

COMPARE & CONTRAST TO

The Snow Child for its portrayal of homesteading in an unforgiving landscape, or *The Paying Guests* for its exploration of historical attitudes towards homosexuality

Room
by Emma Donoghue

FIRST PUBLISHED

2010

LENGTH

401 pages

SETTING

USA

ABOUT THE BOOK

Room is told through the eyes of five-year-old Jack, who lives in a single room with his 'Ma'. Room is no ordinary apartment, however, but a garden shed, adapted to keep them both prisoner. Their captor is 'Old Nick', a man who abducted Ma seven years previously and who is also Jack's biological father. Thanks to his mother's unwavering love and attention, Jack is perfectly happy with his life in Room, unaware that an outside world even exists. Ma, however, fears for Jack's future and devises a terrifying escape plan requiring great bravery from her son.

Real-life abduction stories, such as the notorious Josef Fritzl case inspired the plot for Donoghue's novel. Readers who don't like true crime shouldn't be put off, however, as Donoghue completely avoids the grim sensationalism that such books are often guilty of. Unlike many abduction-themed novels, *Room* shows little interest in entering the psyche of the abductor, who is portrayed as a rather dull peripheral character. Instead, Donoghue focuses entirely on the experience of the captives: particularly Jack, whose narrative captures all the linguistic quirks of a five-year-old. While Jack's narrative subtly conveys the trauma of Ma's experiences through things he sees but does not understand, it equally illustrates the joy and humour in his relationship with Ma. Gripping, moving and surprisingly life-affirming *Room* is ultimately a hymn to maternal love and the bond between mother and child. An international bestseller, the novel appeared on the shortlists for both the Orange Prize and the Man Booker Prize.

ABOUT THE AUTHOR

Emma Donoghue was born in Ireland in 1969 and brought up in a Roman Catholic family. Her father was a literary critic and her mother an English teacher. Her other novels include *Stir Fry; Hood; Slammerkin; Landing; The Sealed Letter; Frog Music* and *The Wonder.* Following the literary success of *Room,* a movie version followed in 2016, for which Donoghue wrote the screenplay. The film was nominated for several Oscars, including Best Adapted Screenplay. Donoghue now lives in Canada.

IN A NUTSHELL

A unique perspective on abduction which is both moving and surprisingly funny

THEMES

Maternal love; parenting; family; societal 'norms'

DISCUSSION QUESTIONS

1/ Discuss the way Jack's narrative captures the linguistics of a small child. Is Jack's voice totally successful/ believable?

2/ Why do you think the author chooses to write the story entirely from Jack's perspective? Would you have welcomed chapters from Ma's point-of-view or does Jack's first person narrative tell us everything we need to know?

3/ Discuss the relationship between Jack and Ma. Is their bond extraordinary or simply a normal mother-son relationship intensified by their confinement?

4/ Ma is endlessly creative in inventing games to encourage her son's development. How difficult do you think it would be to maintain a sense of purpose in Ma's situation? Would this kind of intensive parenting be possible to keep up in the outside world?

5/ Living in Room provokes very different responses in Jack and Ma. Discuss their contrasting feelings about it. Does Jack benefit in any way from growing up in Room?

6/ Discuss Donoghue's treatment of rape in the novel. Is it a sensitive portrayal, or does it play down the horrors of sexual abuse?

7/ Discuss the depiction of 'Old Nick'. What was your overall impression of him? Why do you think Donoghue gives him such a limited role in the novel?

8/ *Room* was inspired by a number of real-life abductions, including the Josef Fritzl case. With this in mind, how does Donoghue prevent her novel from becoming sensationalist or exploitative of real-life victims?

9/ What finally prompts Ma's determination to escape from Room? Do you think she makes the right decision, even though the escape plan puts Jack at risk? What would you have done in her situation?

10/ Discuss the media response to Jack and Ma after their escape. Do you think this is an accurate picture of the way in which the media portray victims of abduction and sexual abuse?

11/ When Jack leaves Room, he finds the outside world a "scary" place. What aspects of it are most challenging for him?

12/ Although Ma is desperate to return to the outside world, she also finds it difficult to adapt to. What are her expectations and in what way does the world disappoint her?

13/ In many ways Jack and Ma's story represents the developmental stages that all mother-child relationships must go through. Discuss.

14/ Would you describe *Room* as an uplifting novel, despite its dark subject matter?

15/ The 2016 movie of *Room*, adapted for the screen by Donoghue, has been widely praised, although some critics felt it lacked the power of the book. If you have seen the movie, how did you feel it compared? Did it bring any fresh aspects to the story?

FURTHER READING

The Wonder, Emma Donoghue
The Light of the Fireflies, Paul Pen
Remember Me Like This, Bret Anthony Johnston
The Girl in the Red Coat, Kate Hamer
The Collector, John Fowles

COMPARE & CONTRAST TO

The Light Between Oceans for its exploration of mother/child relationships, or *The Girls* for its fictional re-imagining of a shocking true crime

The Shock of the Fall
by Nathan Filer

FIRST PUBLISHED

2013

LENGTH

321 pages

SETTING

Bristol, England

ABOUT THE BOOK

The Shock of the Fall is told from the perspective of Matthew Homes, a nineteen-year-old who suffers from schizophrenia. Matthew alternates between enforced stays in psychiatric units and attempting to care for himself within the community. As he does so, he engages in the traumatic but therapeutic act of writing down his life story. It soon becomes clear that the decline in Matthew's mental health is directly related to the death of his Downs Syndrome brother, Simon. As Matthew skirts around the exact details of the event which so haunts him, the reader is left wondering exactly what part he played in the death of his brother.

The unforgettable character of Matthew is one of the elements that make this novel truly exceptional. Despite his sometimes confused perceptions of reality, Matthew's voice has a breathtaking honesty and intimacy. Like Holden Caulfield in *The Catcher in the Rye*, his matter-of-fact observations on life are often brilliantly astute and funny. Matthew's sharp sense of humour throws into relief the poignancy of his fears and anxieties. Looming behind his everyday worries (e.g. whether his grandmother will slip on the ice when she comes to visit him), is his grief and guilt over his brother's death. Matthew's often direct interaction with his reader increases our sense of intimacy with him.

Filer's writing style is inventive and surprising without ever seeming contrived. The use of drawings, lists and quirky typography combine to create the impression of an authentic personal account and reflect the protagonist's fractured sense of identity. Matthew asserts that the only thing he has control over in his life is the way that he tells his own story and, as we would expect, he chooses to tell it in a non-linear way. Aware that memory is not always accurate, he keeps circling back to past events, replaying them in different ways.

The novel examines the themes of grief and mental illness with great sensitivity. Filer explores not only Matthew's grief, but that of his family, who, while still grieving for Simon, are powerless to prevent Matthew's descent into psychosis. Matthew is burdened not only with his illness but with the knowledge of how it hurts the people who love him. His choices are bleak - the side effects of medication and the mind-numbing monotony of life on a psychiatric ward, or the frightening alternative of facing his illness alone. Despite all of this, *The Shock of the Fall* is not an utterly depressing read. The poignancy of the novel's themes are juxtaposed with flashes of optimism and humour, creating just the right balance between light and shade.

ABOUT THE AUTHOR

Nathan Filer is a British author and performance poet. His understanding of the issues surrounding mental illness comes from working as a registered mental health nurse. *The Shock of the Fall* is his debut novel, written after enrolling on a creative writing MA. It was named the Costa Book of the Year in 2013.

IN A NUTSHELL

A quirky and moving portrayal of mental illness from a first-person perspective

THEMES

Mental illness; grief; guilt; loss; sibling relationships

DISCUSSION QUESTIONS

1/ The novel's title refers to an incident in Matthew's childhood, but also represents a great deal more. What do 'the shock' and 'the fall' mean to Matthew?

2/ Is Matthew a reliable narrator? Is his narrative deliberately elusive?

3/ How does Matthew's narrative change as his illness becomes worse?

4/ Discuss the novel's unconventional style (the use of drawings, different fonts etc.). What do you feel this contributed to Matthew's story?

5/ Discuss the factors that contribute to Matthew's mental decline. Do you think anything could have been done to prevent it?

6/ Matthew's narrative often merges past and present events. Did you feel this style was effective or was it confusing?

7/ Discuss Matthew's relationship with his parents. How do they deal with Matthew's illness? Do you think there is any truth in Matthew's claim that his mother is mad?

8/ Discuss Nanny Noo's relationship with Matthew. How does her grandson's illness make her feel?

9/ Matthew says on more than occasion that he is "selfish". Why does he say this? Is there any truth in this statement?

10/ Discuss Matthew's friendship with Jacob. What is it that draws the boys to each other?

11/ Matthew often jokes about his mental illness. Why do you think he does this?

12/ One of Matthew's predominant childhood memories is of watching Annabelle burying her doll. What is the significance of this incident for Anabelle and for Matthew? In what way does Matthew's process of writing compare to Annabelle's ritual?

13/ Matthew says, "I'm a mental patient, not an idiot". Do you think that people suffering from mental illnesses are generally treated like idiots? Does the novel do anything to dissipate the stigma surrounding mental illness?

14/ Did you gain new insight into schizophrenia or mental illness from the novel? What did you make of the author's depiction of psychiatric units, bearing in mind he is a registered mental health nurse?

15/ Discuss the ending of the novel. Did you find a glimmer of hope in it for Matthew's future? Do you think Simon's memorial helps him to find closure?

FURTHER READING

We Used to be Kings, Stewart Foster
Girl, Interrupted, Susanna Kaysen
One Flew Over the Cuckoo's Nest, Ken Kesey
The Curious Incident of the Dog in the Night-time, Mark Haddon
The Silver Linings Playbook, Matthew Quick

COMPARE & CONTRAST TO

The Catcher in the Rye and *We Were Liars* for their quirky adolescent narrations, or *We Are All Completely Beside Ourselves* for the depiction of sibling relationships and guilt

The Snow Child
by Eowyn Ivey

FIRST PUBLISHED

2012

LENGTH

436 pages

SETTING

1920s Alaska

ABOUT THE BOOK

In 1920 a middle-aged couple, Jack and Mabel, move to a homestead in Alaska. The couple have abandoned their easier lives back East as Mabel, devastated by the stillborn birth of her only child, cannot bear to live in proximity to other families with children. The Alaskan landscape, however, is far from welcoming. Jack finds himself losing his battle to farm successfully in the brutal conditions and Mabel succumbs to loneliness and despair. When the first snow falls, Jack and Mabel share a rare moment of togetherness as they build a child out of snow. The next morning the snow child has gone but the couple begin to encounter a free-spirited young girl, Faina, who appears to live alone in the woods. Gradually they entice the girl to become a part of their lives and come to love her as a daughter. It is clear, however, that Faina will never be tamed, and both Jack and Mabel fear that every appearance she makes may be the last.

The Snow Child is a modern retelling of a Russian fairy tale and Ivey beautifully creates the magical and symbolic atmosphere that we associate with the fables of childhood. The novel is also, at times, brutally realistic in its evocation of the beautiful yet unforgiving Alaskan landscape and its impact upon the humans and animals who live there. The pain caused by the childlessness of

Mabel and Jack is poignantly conveyed and, when the intriguing Faina enters their lives, the reader feels both joy on the couple's behalf and an awful sense of foreboding. A haunting story of love and loss, *The Snow Child*, like all the best fairy tales, lingers in the imagination long after the end.

ABOUT THE AUTHOR

Born in 1973, Eowyn Ivey was named after a character in J.R.R. Tolkien's *The Lord of the Rings* and raised in Alaska. She worked as an award-winning reporter before a career change to independent bookseller and author. She studied creative non-fiction at the University of Alaska and is a founding member of Alaska's first state-wide writing centre.

Ivey continues to live in Alaska with her husband and two daughters. They live as sustainable a lifestyle as possible, catching salmon; hunting caribou, moose and bear; growing their own vegetables and harvesting wild berries. *The Snow Child*, Ivey's debut novel, was shortlisted for the Pulitzer Prize for fiction and won the ABA Indies Debut Book of the Year award. Her second novel, *To the Bright Edge of the World*, was published in 2016 and is also set in the Alaskan wilderness.

IN A NUTSHELL

A haunting story of childlessness told with the evocative power of a fable

THEMES

Grief; loss; parenting; maternal love; friendship; the wilderness vs. domesticity

DISCUSSION QUESTIONS

1/ Mabel and Jack are haunted by the loss of their stillborn child years after the event. How do they differ in their response to this loss?

2/ At the beginning of the novel Jack and Mabel both feel that they have failed to make a success of their new life. What makes them feel this way and how does it impact on their relationship?

3/ Mabel longs for a child more than anything. Does this longing stem purely from unfulfilled maternal instincts, or is it also the result of society's expectations of her?

4/ Discuss the roles of George and Esther Benson in the novel. What impact do they have on the lives of Jack and Mabel?

5/ As Jack and Mabel struggle to tame the wilderness of their surroundings, they also try to domesticate Faina. Do their actions reflect their own needs more than Faina's? Are they in any way responsible for her eventual fate?

6/ Discuss the way Mabel develops as the story progresses. How is this reflected in her perception of the homestead and the Alaskan landscape?

7/ Elements of the novel suggest that Faina is a feral child, whilst others seem to indicate she is a magical being. What was your conclusion and why?

8/ How did you feel about the character of Garrett? What initially attracts Garrett to Faina? Is he a positive or malign influence in Faina's life?

9/ The novel includes scenes of brutal realism: particularly images of slayed animals. Why do you think the author includes these images?

10/ Discuss the influence of fairy tales upon *The Snow Child*. Is the novel's mixture of fairy tale and realism a successful combination?

11/ At the beginning of the novel Jack and Mabel mourn their inability to complete their family. How do their perceptions of what constitutes a family change over time?

12/ Throughout the narrative Ivey foreshadows or gives clues to Faina's eventual fate. Discuss these incidents and omens and how they made you feel as you were reading.

13/ What do you think happens to Faina at the end of the novel? Did the novel's epilogue provide a satisfying conclusion to the story?

14/ In what way can Jack and Mabel's experience with Faina be considered a parable of the parenting experience in general?

15/ While their Alaskan lifestyle is gruelling, Jack and Mabel eventually take pleasure in their self-sufficiency. What are the advantages and disadvantages to this kind of lifestyle? Would you be prepared to go 'back to basics' in this way if you had the opportunity?

FURTHER READING

To the Bright Edge of the World, Eowyn Ivey
Some Kind of Fairytale, Graham Joyce
The Bloody Chamber and Other Stories, Angela Carter
Bitter Greens, Kate Forsyth
Wolf Winter, Cecilia Eckback

COMPARE AND CONTRAST TO

The Light Between Oceans for its exploration of the pain of childlessness and maternal love, or *A Place Called Winter* for its portrayal of homesteading in an unforgiving landscape

Station Eleven
by Emily St. John Mandel

FIRST PUBLISHED

2014

LENGTH

384 pages

SETTING

Post-apocalyptic USA

ABOUT THE BOOK

Station Eleven begins when Arthur Leander, a famous actor, dies from a heart attack during a performance of King Lear. That same night, a pandemic wipes out the majority of American citizens. Fifteen years on, the survivors of the pandemic have been forced to go back to basics in a world without technological resources, the internet or even electricity. Among the survivors is Kirsten who, as a child actor, witnessed Arthur Leander's demise. A member of the Travelling Symphony, Kirsten roams from settlement to settlement with her fellow players performing Shakespeare's plays. Their ultimate goal is to reach the Museum of Civilization, which is rumoured to house remnants from the old civilised world. On their travels they encounter dangers, largely in the form of other survivors, some of whom have fallen under the spell of a doomsday prophet.

Refreshingly original, *Station Eleven* is a post-apocalyptic novel for people who do not like post-apocalyptic novels. Although set in the future, there is a timeless feel to this novel as Mandel focusses not so much upon cause as effect. Rather than dwelling on the hows and whys of the end of the world as we know it, Mandel is interested in the way her characters respond to and survive the event. Surprisingly optimistic in its overall tone, the novel suggests that, if all other trappings of civilisation were lost, great art and the endurance of the human spirit would remain a constant.

ABOUT THE AUTHOR

Emily St. John Mandel (St. John is her middle name) is a Canadian novelist. The author was home schooled and then studied dance at the School of Toronto Dance Theater before moving to New York. She is married to the playwright Kevin Mandel and they have a daughter. Mandel's other novels include *Last Night in Montreal*, *The Lola Quartet* and *The Singer's Gun*. *Station Eleven* was a finalist for the National Book Award and won the prestigious Arthur C. Clarke Award for fantasy fiction.

IN A NUTSHELL

A post-apocalyptic novel for readers who would normally prefer Shakespeare

THEMES

Technology; progress & change; the enduring nature of the human spirit & art

DISCUSSION QUESTIONS

1/ Each one of the major characters is linked to Arthur Leander in some way. Discuss the intricate connections between the characters and the influence Arthur has had upon them.

2/ What was your opinion of Arthur as a character? What does he have in common with his dramatic alter ego, King Lear? In what way do his conflicting feelings about the island where he grew up influence his behaviour? Why do you think the author chooses to begin the story with Arthur's death?

3/ The novel has a complex structure, constantly shifting in viewpoint and bouncing back and forth between pre-and post-pandemic timeframes. What does this add to the reading experience? Did you enjoy each character's perspective equally or did you have a favourite?

4/ The motto of the Travelling Symphony is "survival is insufficient". What is the group's motivation for continuing to travel and perform? Are there other examples in the novel of individuals striving to do more than simply survive?

5/ The repertoire of the Travelling Symphony consists mainly of Shakespeare's plays, as they go down best with audiences. Why do you think this is? What is it about Shakespeare's work that still strikes a chord with audiences hundreds of years after the Bard's death?

6/ Arthur's relationship with his childhood friend, Victoria, remains something of a mystery. Why does Arthur continue to write deeply personal letters to her long after she ceases to reply? What did you think of Victoria's decision to publish Arthur's letters?

7/ Why did Mandel choose the title *Station Eleven* for her novel? What parallels are there between Miranda's fictional world and Mandel's?

8/ The Prophet, as Tyler comes to be known, compares the Georgia flu to the great flood, casting himself in the role of Noah. Discuss the sinister path religion seems to take after the pandemic. What elements of Tyler's upbringing influence him to become the head of a doomsday cult?

9/ The author makes reference to several real epidemics such as SARS, as well as the fictional Georgia flu. Do you think a future pandemic is a distinct possibility? Placed in a similar situation to the characters in the novel, would you want to survive if your family and friends had all perished?

10/ Following the pandemic, certain items of ephemera become permanent reminders of the old world. Discuss the objects the characters become attached to and the totemic significance these items take on.

11/ Compare Kirsten and Clerk's very different attitudes towards remembering the old world. Do you think remembering your history is essential, or is it sometimes necessary to block out the past in order to go on? What do you think may have happened to Kirsten in her first year on the road?

12/ Jeevan Chaudhary cannot help but compare his situation to the many apocalyptic disaster movies he has seen. What does the novel have in common with typical 'end of the world' movies and how does it differ?

13/ Many of the younger characters in the novel are preoccupied with the idea that the internet "might still be out there somehow." If the internet ceased to exist in reality would you mourn its loss? Do any benefits emerge for the characters when they are forced to go back to basics?

14/ Kirsten's few memories of the old world are of lights, air conditioning and refrigerators, and the novel ends as she and the Travelling Symphony make their way towards the settlement which appears to have generated electric light. What does electricity represent to Kirsten? Do you think the author is suggesting that society will gradually re-establish everything that has been lost?

15/ If apocalyptic fiction is not your usual milieu, has reading *Station Eleven* encouraged you to explore the genre further?

FURTHER READING

The Lola Quartet, Emily St. John Mandel
The End of the World Running Club, Adrian J. Walker
I Am Legend, Richard Matheson
Oryx and Crake, Margaret Atwood
The Road, Cormac McCarthy

COMPARE AND CONTRAST TO

The Heart Goes Last for its opposing vision of the role of technology in the future

The Storied Life of A.J. Fikry
by Gabrielle Zevin

FIRST PUBLISHED

2014

LENGTH

320 PAGES

SETTING

USA

ABOUT THE BOOK

A.J. Fikry is an independent bookstore owner on a small American island. Already considered cold and snobbish by the local community, he becomes positively reclusive after the death of his wife, losing interest in life, other people and even books. The direction of his life takes a dramatic turn, however, when he discovers a two-year-old girl, Maya, abandoned in the children's section of his store. Maya worms her way into A.J.'s heart and the bookstore owner adopts her. In the process of his steep learning curve as a father, A.J. comes to realise that once you start caring about one thing, it opens up your heart to others. Maya's arrival prompts him to breathe new life into the bookstore, build links with his community and even find love second time around.

The Storied Life is a life-affirming novel which explores love, loss and second chances. Moving and poignant, particularly in its treatment of the power of parental love, it is also very funny in parts. Perhaps most importantly, this book is written for the benefit of true book lovers. Each chapter of the novel is prefaced by a short story recommendation by A.J. for his daughter. A.J.'s choices reveal a great deal about his life and emotions, illustrating the power of fiction to express the contents of our hearts. *The*

Storied Life explores the reasons why we read and celebrates how books can unite us, elevate us and even make us better people. Book group members will enjoy its depiction of book club meetings, particularly the crime enthusiasts' group, where a 'no firearms' policy has to be introduced, as the discussions become so heated. The novel also makes a convincing case for the importance of small bookstores and, in the process, raises interesting debates about the future of the book: paper versus e-readers, independent sellers versus online etc. It would be hard to find another book more ideal for reading group discussions.

* For those confused over the title the novel was published as *The Collected Works of A.J. Fikry* in the U.K.

ABOUT THE AUTHOR

Gabrielle Zevin is an American author and screenwriter, born in 1977. She studied English at Harvard before beginning her writing career as a music critic. Zevin co-wrote the screenplay for the film, 'Conversations with Other Women' starring Helena Bonham Carter. She is also the author of a series of Young Adult novels. Her adult fiction includes *Margarettown* and *The Hole We're In*. Zevin's fiction covers a wide range of unusual subjects from amnesia, to the afterlife, to female soldiers in Iraq. Her writing style is distinctive for its quirky humour.

IN A NUTSHELL

A hymn to the joys of reading and connecting with others

THEMES

The joy of reading; friendship; love; loss; parenting; community; the future of books

DISCUSSION QUESTIONS

1/ Who was your favourite character and why? Did your opinion of any of the characters change as the novel progressed?

2/ A.J.'s character undergoes dramatic changes in the course of the novel. Two incidents in particular highlight this – his decision to expand the store's children section and his use of the e-reader in hospital. What do these episodes tell us about A.J.?

3/ Discuss the connection between love and loss in the novel. How did you feel about the way A.J. and Amelia's story mirrored events in *The Late Bloomer*?

4/ Did you empathise with the character of Marian, or did you find her decision to leave her child and end her own life unforgivable?

5/ What did you think of Ismay's decision to keep the circumstances surrounding Marian's death a secret? Would Maya benefit from knowing the identity of her biological father?

6/ Why does A.J. give Maya the middle name 'Tamerlane'? What does this say about his altered values?

7/ *The Late Bloomer* celebrates finding love late in life, as both A.J. and Ismay find love again after the death of their first spouses. What are the advantages of a more 'mature' love?

8/ Discuss the scene where Daniel Parish is killed in a car crash and Ismay's thought processes leading up to this moment. Do you think Ismay deliberately parks recklessly, knowing what may happen?

9/ Do you think that Maya's life would have been very different if she had not been left in a bookstore? Does A.J.'s literary influence shape her, or is she destined to become a writer anyway?

10/ In his review of 'The Luck of Roaring Camp', A.J. points out that we can respond very differently to books depending on the life stage we are at when reading them. Do you think this is true? Have you ever re-read a story or novel and responded very differently to it second time around? If so why?

11/ A.J. believes that you can glean everything you need to know about a person by finding out their favourite book. Is it true that our choice of reading matter expresses our personalities? What is your favourite book and what do you think this says about you?

12/ Lambiase is turned off reading when he is a child through negative experiences at school. How important do you think school literature classes are in shaping our attitudes to reading? At what stage in life did you learn to love books?

13/ Leonora Ferris, the real author of *The Late Bloomer,* claims that it doesn't matter whether her story is true or not as long as it touches people. Do you agree? Would you feel defrauded to discover a memoir you had read was actually fiction? What does this episode say about the emotional truth of fiction?

14/ The novel celebrates the role of the independent bookshop within the literary world. Do such stores stand a chance in today's cutthroat financial climate? Is A.J. right to fear the introduction of the e-reader, or is there a place for both?

15/ Did you anticipate the ending of the novel? How do you foresee the futures of Amelia, Maya and Island Books? Did you find the conclusion bleak or uplifting?

FURTHER READING

The Shadow of the Wind, Carlos Ruiz Zafon
Mr Penumbra's 24-Hour Bookstore, Robin Sloan
The Thirteenth Tale, Diane Setterfield
The Little Coffee Shop of Kabul, Deborah Rodriguez
The Unlikely Pilgrimage of Harold Fry, Rachel Joyce

COMPARE AND CONTRAST TO

The Guernsey Literary and Potato Peel Pie Society for its celebration of the power of literature, or *A Man Called Ove* for its portrayal of a man who is forced to engage with the world

The Sympathizer
by Viet Thanh Nguyen

FIRST PUBLISHED

2015

LENGTH

384 pages

SETTING

Vietnam and the USA, 1975 onwards

ABOUT THE BOOK

The sympathizer of Viet Thanh Nguyen's novel is an unnamed narrator whose story takes the form of a confession. The illegitimate child of a Vietnamese teenage maid and a French Catholic priest, he has been trained by the CIA and works as an aide to a General of the South Vietnamese army. Unbeknown to his employer, he is also a communist undercover agent, assigned to spy on the General.

The narrator's account begins in the final days of the Vietnam War, leading up to the Fall of Saigon in April 1975. As American troops withdraw from Vietnam, leaving the South Vietnamese people to their fate, the communist army takes control of the country. Realising that it is no longer safe to stay in Vietnam, the General decides it is time to leave for the USA and charges the narrator with the task of deciding who will get a seat on the last plane out. The narrator saves himself, along with his best friend Bon, who also works for the CIA and has no idea that the narrator is a communist agent. In Los Angeles the narrator takes a job at a Californian university and becomes involved in an ill-fated Vietnam War movie project. At the same time, he continues to observe the General and sends coded messages back to his communist contact in Vietnam. Things start to get messy, however, when the General, who is planning to invade Vietnam and seize back power from the communists, begins to suspect that his network has been infiltrated by a spy. In an attempt to throw the General off the scent, the narrator accuses an innocent man of being the mole and helps to assassinate him. One murder inevitably leads to another, and the narrator soon finds himself haunted by the ghosts of those he has betrayed. Inevitably, he begins to crack under the strain of leading a double life and deceiving those around him.

Viet Thanh Nguyen's debut novel won not only the 2016 Pulitzer Prize for Fiction but also the Andrew Carnegie Medal for Excellence in Fiction, the 2015 Center for Fiction First Novel Prize and the Asian/Pacific American Award for Literature in Fiction. The novel was also singled out on more than thirty influential best-book-of-the-year lists. A great deal of the critical praise this novel received was for the fresh (i.e. Vietnamese) perspective it brings to the representation of the Vietnam War. While there has been no shortage of representations of this conflict in film or fiction, almost all of them have been from an American perspective. The American appropriation of the Vietnam War experience is humorously highlighted in Nguyen's novel when the narrator becomes involved in the making of 'The Hamlet' (a thinly veiled take-off of Francis Ford Coppola's 'Apocalypse Now'). While the narrator completely fails in his attempts to get the director to portray the Vietnamese as real human beings, Nguyen redresses the balance in his novel. In particular, he reminds readers that, while the USA was licking its wounds after failing to achieve victory in the war, the impact upon the Vietnamese was much worse. Strategically beginning his story with the American withdrawal from Vietnam before the Fall of Saigon, Nguyen describes the sense of abandonment experienced by the South Vietnamese, the fate of the refugees and the experiences of those sent to communist re-education camps.

As well as putting the Vietnamese back into the Vietnam War, Nguyen situates the conflict within the wider history of Vietnam. The novel's conflicted narrator finds his sense of identity increasingly divided as he sympathises with both the communists and the people he spies upon. In this way he embodies Vietnam itself: a country whose psyche has been fractured by repeated invasion and colonisation. The narrator's precarious sense of self is further threatened by his observations of the way he and his people are perceived and represented as stereotypes within American culture.

Like most hugely ambitious works of fiction, *The Sympathizer* isn't easy to categorise. A Vietnam War novel, an espionage thriller, a political satire, a coming-of-age tale and a powerful portrayal of the immigrant experience, it also has unmistakably Shakespearean undertones (think 'Hamlet' meets 'Macbeth' with dashes of comedy). Although not the easiest of reads, this exciting contribution to Asian American literature is well-worth the effort.

ABOUT THE AUTHOR

Viet Thanh Nguyen was born in Ban Me Thuot, Vietnam. In 1975, when he was only four years old, the Vietnamese communist army took over the village where he lived. He and his family fled the country and stayed in refugee camps, first in Guam and then in Pennsylvania. As part of a sponsorship scheme for Vietnamese refugees, Nguyen was separated from his parents and sent to live with a white host family. He was reunited with his birth family in 1978 when they moved to San Jose, California. Here, his parents opened one of the first Vietnamese grocery stores in the city.

Nguyen graduated from UC Berkeley with degrees in English and Ethnic Studies and stayed on to complete a Ph.D. in English literature. He then moved to Los Angeles for a position at the University of Southern California where he still teaches. An associate Professor of English and American Studies and Ethnicity, Nguyen is particularly interested in exploring the way Asians and Asian-Americans are represented in American culture.

Although Nguyen has written short stories for various publications, *The Sympathizer* was his first novel. His non-fiction titles include *Race and Resistance: Literature and Politics in Asian America* and *Nothing Ever Dies: Vietnam and the Memory of War*.

IN A NUTSHELL

A powerful exploration of Vietnamese cultural identity

THEMES

Exile; cultural identity; racial stereotyping; political corruption;

fraternity; memory; the power of language

DISCUSSION QUESTIONS

1/ The novel begins with the opening sentences, "I am a spy, a sleeper, a spook, a man of two faces. Perhaps not surprisingly, I am also a man of two minds." In what respects is the narrator divided? How does his identity reflect the history and identity of Vietnam?

2/ Did you find the first-person voice of the narrator engaging? Why, or why not? Did you empathise with him?

3/ Is the narrator's ability to sympathise with both sides beneficial to him, or a burden? How does he compare to those characters who only see one side of a situation? What does Nguyen suggest is the inherent danger of an unambiguous point of view?

4/ *The Sympathizer* is a book of many different genres – espionage thriller; immigrant novel; social and political satire, and war novel. Did this blend of different genres work for you? Which section of the novel did you enjoy most and why?

5/ Through the experiences of his South Vietnamese characters, Nguyen presents a powerful portrait of how it feels to be an immigrant. Discuss the experience of the refugees from the moment they leave their country to their resettlement in the USA. How does exile impact on the characters' sense of identity? How are they treated in the USA?

6/ Discuss the humorous observations the narrator makes about American culture. What does he suggest are its greatest absurdities? Is he completely immune to the lure of American culture himself?

7/ Discuss the different ways in which the Vietnamese are misrepresented or rendered invisible in the making of the movie 'The Hamlet'. Do you think this is an accurate reflection of the way ethnic minorities, including East Asians, are portrayed by Hollywood?

8/ Nguyen unapologetically based 'The Hamlet' on Francis Ford

Coppola's iconic Vietnam War film, 'Apocalypse Now'. In what ways does the Auteur distort the Vietnam narrative to fit a particular vision of American national identity? If you have seen 'Apocalypse Now' do you feel that Coppola does the same? Do you think it is true that movies have the power to shape our ideas about historical events?

9/ Discuss the narrator's attitudes towards women and sex. Does the author critique this viewpoint in any way? Did you feel the female characters in the novel were fully-fleshed?

10/ Discuss the character of Claude. Did your feelings change towards him as the novel progressed? How does his character contribute to the novel's implied critique of the USA's torture program in Vietnam and following 9/11? Were you fully aware of the extent of the USA's torture programs before reading the novel? Is torture ever a justifiable interrogation technique, or should it always be considered a war crime?

11/ Claude gives the narrator two gifts: a rucksack and a copy of *Asian Communism and the Oriental Mode of Destruction*. What is the symbolic significance of these gifts and how does the narrator subvert their intended purpose?

12/ Discuss the dynamics of the relationship between the narrator, Bon and Man. What is their friendship based upon? Is their bond the only glimmer of hope in an otherwise bleak story?

13/ The narrator's eventual disillusionment with the communist revolution raises universal questions about power and human nature. Discuss the many forms that corruption takes in the novel. Do you think that the human tendency to abuse power will always stand in the way of a revolution that truly benefits the people?

14/ At the end of the novel Bon and the narrator face a dangerous journey as they join the boat people. Discuss the associations the narrator suggests 'boat people' holds as a term. What effect does this kind of categorisation have upon Western perceptions of refugees? Are there any parallels with the current refugee crises?

15/ James Grainger describes *The Sympathizer* as, "A tremendously funny novel, stripped bare of the liberal humanist pieties of so many novels of immigration, exile and foreign conflict." Did the mix of harrowing subject matter with humorous observations work for you?

FURTHER READING

The Quiet American, Graham Greene
Invisible Man, Ralph Ellison
The Sorrow of War, Bao Ninh
A Good Scent from a Strange Mountain, Robert Olen Butler
Native Speaker, Chang-Rae Lee

COMPARE AND CONTRAST TO

The Year of the Runaways for its portrayal of the immigrant experience, or *Everything I Never Told You* for the exploration of Asian stereotyping

The Tiger's Wife
by Téa Obreht

FIRST PUBLISHED

2011

LENGTH

338 pages

SETTING

The former Yugoslavia, present and past

ABOUT THE BOOK

Natalia is a Serbian doctor on a road trip across the former Yugoslavia. Her mission is to reach a monastery in the village of Brejevina where she is to inoculate children who have been orphaned by the war. On the journey, however, she learns that her beloved grandfather has died in an unfamiliar location, not far from her destination. From this point, her aid mission is twinned with a quest to investigate the strange circumstances surrounding her grandfather's death.

To reflect the dual nature of her journey, the novel splits into two timelines as Natalia's experiences are interrupted by memories of the many fabulous stories her grandfather told her. She comes to the conclusion that the answer to the mystery surrounding his death "lies between two stories: the story of the tiger's wife, and the story of the deathless man". Her grandfather claimed to have encountered both mysterious figures during his lifetime. The tiger's wife, a deaf Muslim woman, was a resident of his home village of Galina, which was stalked by an escaped tiger. Unlike the rest of the villagers who feared the tiger, the Muslim woman formed a special understanding with the creature, leading her neighbours to gossip that she was secretly wedded to it. The deathless man, meanwhile, was an immortal who appeared whenever death was imminent to drink coffee with those about to die. Having always assumed that these stories were fables, Natalia is forced to reassess them and how they relate to her grandfather's fate.

Through combining Natalia's present-day worldly observations with fable-inspired stories, Obreht hits upon an ingenious way to explore the troubled history of the Balkans. Her narrative deliberately avoids using specific place names and never directly refers to atrocities, such as the massacres of Brcko and Srebenica, which took place in the wars during the 1990s. All this is implicit, however, in the fables told by Natalia's grandfather and in Natalia's observations of a country left wounded and divided by war. The novel's matryoshka-like narrative, combining stories within stories, is more than just a clever stylistic feature. The complex non-linear plot also highlights the near impossibility of recounting Yugoslavia's tangled history in a straightforward narrative. As *The Tiger's Wife* is ultimately an elegy for Yugoslavia, it is a credit to Obreht's richly imaginative style of storytelling that she turns such bleak subject matter into a novel that is a joy to read. Quirky and lyrical, her narrative demonstrates the power folklore holds to express the inexpressible.

ABOUT THE AUTHOR

Téa Obreht was born Téa Bajraktarevic in Belgrade, Yugoslavia (now Serbia) in 1985. When she was seven, her family left Yugoslavia just as war was breaking out. They lived in Cyprus and Egypt before finally settling in the U.S. when Téa was 12. As she had no father in her life, Téa became particularly close to her maternal grandfather and took his surname when he died, officially changing it to Obreht. At the age of 24, she was named on the *New Yorker's* list of top 20 young writers in recognition of the talent displayed in her published short stories. *The Tiger's Wife* was completed on a creative writing course at Cornell University. When the debut novel went on to win the 2011 Orange Prize for Fiction, Obreht became the youngest writer to receive the award. The author currently lives in New York.

IN A NUTSHELL

A richly imaginative fable about the Balkan wars

THEMES

War; storytelling; family; loss; death; rationality versus faith; violence; prejudice

DISCUSSION QUESTIONS

1/ The narrative juxtaposes Natalia's matter-of-fact narration with fantastical folk tales. Which did you prefer and why?

2/ Discuss the role of storytelling in the novel. What function does it serve?

3/ *The Tiger's Wife* has a Russian doll-like structure, layering stories within stories. Did you find this structure effective or distracting? What does the technique do to the pace of the story? Is a strong sense of narrative drive important to you in a novel?

4/ Did the lack of specific geographical and time references in the novel frustrate you? Why do you think the author chose to avoid referring to specific events or places in the novel?

5/ Natalia has lived her life under the shadow of war and then in its aftermath. How has this shaped the identity of her generation?

6/ The villagers of Galina live in fear of the escaped tiger that circles the area. On a wider level, what do you think their fear of him represents? Why does the reaction of Natalia's grandfather differ from that of the other villagers?

7/ How did you interpret the relationship between Luka's wife and the tiger? Why do the villagers of Galina become so fixated on the nature of their relationship?

8/ The author provides backstories for many of her minor characters, including Luka, Darisa and the apothecary. Did the revelation of their histories make you feel any more sympathetic towards them as characters?

9/ While the stories of Natalia's grandfather have a magical quality, they also frequently feature images of violence and cruelty. Discuss some of these episodes and what you think they represent.

10/ When he has dinner with the deathless man, Natalia's grandfather tries to persuade his companion to inform their waiter of his imminent death. Do you think Natalia's grandfather is right to believe that the waiter would want to know his fate? Would you want to know if death was around the corner, or would you rather remain blissfully ignorant?

11/ The novel is littered with bodies (Natalia's grandfather, the deathless man, the cousin in the suitcase, the remains of Darisa) and one of the dilemmas the characters face is how best to dispose of them. What lengths do the characters go to in order to appease or honour the dead? Why does Natalia volunteer to take on the role of the Mora?

12/ Discuss the tension between Natalia's belief in science and rationality and her encounters with Balkan superstition. What do you think the author is trying to say about the role of superstition in peoples' lives?

13/ Obreht's fictional world deliberately challenges the notion of rigid boundaries. Discuss the way the author breaks down boundaries between life and death, animals and humans, and reality and fiction in her novel.

14/ Although *The Tiger's Wife* is a novel about war, Obreht never directly describes warfare. In what other ways does she convey the violence of war and its aftermath? What advantages does a fable about war have over a realistic portrayal of the same subject matter? Are there any disadvantages?

15/ The author left Yugoslavia as a child, just before the conflicts of the 1990s really began. Does it matter that her representation of the death of Yugoslavia is the product of imagination rather than experience?

FURTHER READING

Girl at War, Sara Novic
Seven Terrors, Selvedin Avdic
The Hired Man, Aminatta Forna
Life of Pi, Yann Martel
The Little Red Chairs, Edna O'Brien

COMPARE AND CONTRAST TO

The Snow Child or *The Underground Railroad* for their blending of the real and the fabulous

The Turn of the Screw
by Henry James

FIRST PUBLISHED

1898

LENGTH

78 pages

SETTING

Nineteenth century England

ABOUT THE BOOK

First published in 1898, *The Turn of the Screw* was extraordinarily ahead of its time and remains one of the most influential ghost stories today. Henry James's Gothic masterpiece has become the benchmark against which all following horror fiction has been compared. The novella's legacy can also still be traced in the popularity of horror movies centring upon demonically possessed children ('The Exorcist', 'The Omen' and many, many others).

James's story is narrated by a nameless young woman, who is hired by the rich uncle of two children to work as a governess at a remote country estate. When the narrator arrives at Bly, the country house, she is surprised to find that her only adult company is the housekeeper. She is, however, instantly captivated by Flora, her beautiful and agreeable young charge. Alarm bells start to ring for the Governess when she learns that Flora's ten-year-old brother, Miles, has been expelled from his boarding school for unknown reasons. The narrator broods over what crime Miles could have committed but when he arrives home her fears are allayed, as he turns out to be just as beautiful and charming as his sister. Soon, the Governess begins to see two sinister figures lurking around the house and she comes to believe they are the ghosts of Peter Quint, a former servant and Miss Jessel, the previous governess. When Flora and Miles claim that they are unable to see these spirit manifestations, the Governess comes to the conclusion that the ghosts intend to corrupt her charges and she engages in a battle to protect their innocence.

Much of the power of *The Turn of the Screw* lies in its ambiguity. The story is open to several different interpretations and, as a consequence, critics have heatedly debated its meaning. Is it really a tale of the supernatural, or a portrait of a deranged mind? Whichever interpretation you choose, the implications are just as frightening.

ABOUT THE AUTHOR

Henry James was a novelist and literary critic. Born in New York in 1843, he spent much of his adult life in England and became a British subject in 1915, the year before he died. One of the greatest American exponents of the nineteenth century novel, his most famous works included *The Golden Bowl*, *The Wings of the Dove*, *Daisy Miller* and *The Portrait of a Lady*. James was great friends with fellow American novelist, Edith Wharton. He never married and recent biographers have suggested he may have been homosexual.

IN A NUTSHELL

A creepy gothic story that set the benchmark for future tales of the supernatural

THEMES

Many of the themes of this novel are debatable, depending upon how you interpret the story. They may include innocence vs. corruption; class; gender roles; the power of the unconscious; mental illness and sexual repression.

DISCUSSION QUESTIONS

1/ What is the purpose of the story's Prologue. Why do you think James chooses to begin *The Turn of the Screw* in this way?

2/ The protagonist of *The Turn of the Screw* is known only as the Governess. Why do you think the author chose not to give his main character a name? Is she a trustworthy narrator? Did your assessment of her reliability change as the story progressed?

3/ In what ways does the story reflect the preoccupations and restrictions of Victorian society?

4/ The Governess quickly oversteps professional boundaries in her relationship with Flora and Miles. How did you feel about the intensity of her feelings towards the children? Does she display natural motherly instincts or something more troubling?

5/ As *The Turn of the Screw* progresses, the misbehaviour of Miles and Flora leads the Governess to believe that they have fallen under an evil influence. Is this the only interpretation of the children's behaviour? How much experience of children do you think the Governess has? Could it be that her notions of childhood innocence are unrealistic?

6/ One of the Governess's major preoccupations is to protect the innocence of her young charges. What is her definition of innocence? Do you think her fear of corruption is fuelled by an incident in her own past?

7/ The Governess fears that the children have seen "things terrible and unguessable". What do you think she means by this? How much do you think the children have really seen and heard?

8/ When he hires the Governess, the children's uncle makes it clear that he does not want her to contact him regarding their care. Why do you think the Governess so rigidly adheres to these instructions, despite her concerns? What would you have done in her situation?

9/ In 1938 the critic Edmund Wilson suggested that the Governess is a sexually repressed woman, driven mad by her hidden desires. Can you think of any parts of the text which seem to support this theory?

10/ The narrative makes it clear that, although Peter Quint became a powerful figure at Bly while he was alive, he was not a 'gentleman'. Can the story be read as a cautionary tale about the rise of the working classes?

11/ One of the central mysteries of the plot is the cause of Miles's expulsion from boarding school and, in the final chapter, Miles finally admits to the Governess that he was expelled because he "said things" to students he liked. What do you think he said? Were his actions necessarily prompted by his association with Peter Quint?

12/ Just before Miles dies he cries out, "Peter Quint – you devil!" Is he addressing the ghost of Peter Quint or the Governess? How did you interpret the events surrounding Miles's death?

13/ The power of Henry James's story lies in its ambiguity, as the reader is left to decide whether Miles and Flora really were possessed by evil spirits, or whether the Governess kills Miles while in the grip of a mental illness. Which do you think is the more frightening interpretation?

14/ The demonic possession of children is still a popular theme today, particularly in horror movies. Why do you think this idea strikes such a chord with us? What instinctive fears does it play upon?

15/ Has *The Turn of the Screw* stood the test of time as a ghost story? Did you find it genuinely frightening? What is it about tales of the supernatural that we find so disturbing?

FURTHER READING

The Yellow Wallpaper, Charlotte Perkins Gilman
The Haunting of Hill House, Shirley Jackson
The Little Stranger, Sarah Waters
The Grownup, Gillian Flynn
Slade House, David Mitchell

COMPARE AND CONTRAST TO

The Woman in Black and *The Loney* – (how has this classic influenced these later gothic novels?) or *The Catcher in the Rye* for the narrator's preoccupation with preserving childhood innocence.

The Underground Railroad by Colson Whitehead

FIRST PUBLISHED

2016

LENGTH

306 pages

SETTING

1850s America

ABOUT THE BOOK

One of the most eagerly anticipated novels of 2016, Colson Whitehead's *The Underground Railroad* was released a month early to meet public demand. Some of the excitement over the novel was generated by praise from celebrities. Oprah Winfrey chose it for her hugely popular Book Club while Barack Obama also recommended the novel to the American public. Whitehead's novel is much more, however, than a literary flavour-of-the-month. Literary critics have agreed that *The Underground Railroad* is one of the most remarkable novels to tackle the legacy of American slavery since Toni Morrison's *Beloved*.

The Underground Railroad begins with a prologue recounting the story of Ajarry. Ajarry is an African woman who is kidnapped, sold into slavery and shipped to America where she is sold on repeatedly, ending her days on the Randall cotton plantation in Georgia. Years later Ajarry's daughter, Mabel, has escaped the plantation leaving her own daughter, Cora, to fend for herself. Treated as a pariah by the other slaves and raped when she reaches puberty, Cora still refuses to contemplate taking the same risk as her mother, until she is singled out by the plantation's sadistic owner as his next concubine. At this point she agrees to make a bid for freedom with Caesar, a fellow slave. With the help of underground railroad agents, Cora and Caesar begin a quest to find a state that will offer them liberty and equality. It soon becomes apparent, however, that while some American states appear more benevolent than others, each one seeks to control African Americans, from capping how much they can earn to limiting population numbers. Also threatening their quest for freedom are the slave patrollers who have the jurisdiction to search for and capture runaway slaves, even within the free states. Pursuing Cora throughout her journey is the infamous slave catcher, Arnold Ridgeway, who, having failed to recapture Cora's mother years earlier, makes retrieving her daughter his life's mission.

One of the reasons for the buzz around this novel is the startlingly original way in which the author treats his subject matter. As Whitehead has said in interview, "I'm dealing with serious race issues, but I'm not handling them in a way that people expect." While the story is inspired by genuine nineteenth century slave narratives, it is also strongly influenced by Jonathan Swift's *Gulliver's Travels,* as well as introducing elements of magic realism. The result is a truly extraordinary mixture of realism, satire and speculative fiction. Imagine, if you can, *Twelve Years a Slave,* meets *The Adventures of Huckleberry Finn* meets *One Hundred Years of Solitude* and you might be close to the mood of Whitehead's novel. At the centre of this surreal mix is the author's concept of the underground railroad (the network of activists who helped runaway slaves) as a literal railway with a track and stations hidden underground. Whitehead then extends this fantastical idea by providing the railroad with the properties of a time machine. While everything that Cora observes on her journey is based, at least loosely, on historical events, some of the incidents covered (such as the use of eugenics and medical experimentation on African Americans) did not take place until the first half of the twentieth century. Whitehead draws attention to the slippery quality of time in his novel by introducing obvious anachronisms, such as a skyscraper erected in the middle of nineteenth century South Carolina.

The overall effect of Whitehead's curious mix of genres is to express much more than can be said in a strictly realist novel. On one level, Cora's story brilliantly conveys the emotional and physical horrors of slavery. On a wider level, her fantastical journey becomes a metaphor for the experiences of all African Americans from slavery to the present day. In describing the various forms of racism witnessed by Cora on her travels, the author highlights the way in which one form of racial oppression has simply been exchanged for another. In doing so, he creates a damning portrait of America's past and also asks some very uncomfortable questions about its present attitude to race.

ABOUT THE AUTHOR

Colson Whitehead was born in 1969 and grew up in Manhattan. He was educated at private schools with a mostly white studentship. After graduating from Harvard in 1991 he worked as a freelance journalist before becoming an author. As a novelist, Whitehead has become known for his unpredictable and experimental style, which is often used to explore the U.S.A.'s attitude towards race. His first novel, *The Intuitionist*, was published in 1999 and focuses upon the life of a female African American elevator inspector in mid-twentieth century Manhattan. Other works have included a novel about the 'steel-driving' man of American folk lore (*John Henry Days*), a coming-of-age novel set in the 1980s (*Sag Harbor*), a post-apocalyptic zombie thriller (*Zone One*) and a book about a World Series poker player (*The Noble Hustle; Poker, Beef Jerky & Death*).

Whitehead has been a finalist for a number of prestigious literary prizes, including the Pen/ Hemingway, the National Book Critics' Circle Award, the Los Angeles Times Fiction Award and the Pulitzer Prize. In 2002 he was awarded the MacArthur Fellowship grant. Otherwise known as the 'Genius Grant', the MacArthur Fellowship is awarded to recognise an individual's "originality, insight, and potential." His reviews, essays and short stories have appeared in *The New York Times*, *The New Yorker*, *Harpers* and *Granta*. The author continues to live in Manhattan and teaches creative writing at several universities. He is married to a literary agent and has two children.

IN A NUTSHELL

A slave narrative with a unique twist

THEMES

Racism; the abuse of power; freedom; endurance; community; history; eugenics

DISCUSSION QUESTIONS

1/ *The Underground Railroad* includes the narratives of three generations of women: Ajarry, Mabel and Cora. What do these characters have in common and how do they differ? Does the difference in their fates suggest progress down the generations?

2/ How did you feel about Mabel's decision to run away from the Randall plantation without her daughter? Is Cora's hatred of her mother justified?

3/ Discuss the way Cora is treated by the other slaves on the Randall plantation after she is abandoned by her mother. Did this negative portrayal of the black community surprise you? What point do you think the author is making? Are there any positive representations of community in the novel?

4/ Although Cora is victimised by others she never behaves like a victim. Discuss the ways in which she fights against the different types of oppression she encounters.

5/ Cora's story is told through a third-person narrator. Why do you think the author chose a third-person narrative for his subject matter? What impact does it have on the tone of the novel? Did the narrative work for you or would you have preferred a first-person narration?

6/ Discuss the different forms of racism Cora encounters in the American states she passes through. What is this prejudice driven by? Which state, in your opinion, was the worst in its violation of human rights?

7/ While Cora's perspective dominates, *The Underground Railroad* includes narratives from the point-of-view of a range of other characters. Why do you think the author includes the stories of relatively minor characters such as Dr Stevens and Ethel Wells? Did they add anything to the novel?

8/ Discuss the author's use of deliberate anachronisms and magic realism in his story. How do these elements allow the author to express things that could not be conveyed in a strictly realist novel? How did you feel about the combination of realism and fantasy? Is it appropriate for Whitehead's subject matter?

9/ Discuss the way in which the control of language and literacy is shown to be a powerful tool in maintaining the oppression of African Americans.

10/ Ridgeway's guiding philosophy is a belief in "the American spirit". What does he mean by this? How does his belief relate to the references to American Indians in the novel?

11/ One of Cora's jobs in South Carolina is to work as a live exhibit in the Museum of Natural Wonders. What does this experience say about America's attitude to its national history?

12/ In the paternalistic state of South Carolina, Cora discovers that black women are being sterilised without their consent, while black men are the unwitting subjects of research into syphilis. Does it surprise you that these fictional incidents were based on historical fact? Is state control of population numbers ever ethically acceptable?

13/ Discuss the parallels the novel draws between Cora's experience in North Carolina and the regime of Nazi Germany. Can you think of more recent events which also bear a similarity to the atmosphere of racial hatred and fear Cora finds in North Carolina?

14/ By the closing pages of the novel Cora still has a long way to travel before she reaches freedom. Did you interpret the ending in an optimistic light?

15/ Have you read any other fictional or factual books about African American slavery? If so, do you feel that *The Underground*

Railroad makes a new and significant contribution to this canon of work? Do you feel that the novel gave you a deeper understanding of the slave experience?

FURTHER READING

Beloved, Toni Morrison
Homegoing, Yaa Gyasi
The Sellout, Paul Beatty
Incidents in the Life of a Slave Girl, Harriet Jacobs
One Hundred Years of Solitude, Gabriel Garcia Marquez

COMPARE AND CONTRAST TO

The Invention of Wings for its depiction of the slave experience, or *The Tiger's Wife* for the use of magic realism in recounting historical horrors

We Are All Completely Beside Ourselves by Karen Joy Fowler

FIRST PUBLISHED

2013

LENGTH

320 pages

SETTING

USA, 1970s to the near-present

ABOUT THE BOOK

It is hard to summarise this extraordinary novel without revealing spoilers. About a quarter of a way through the story, the narrator makes a revelation that completely shifts the reader's perception of events. The nature of this surprise will not be revealed in this summary, although readers who really do not want to know would do well to avoid all reviews and even the blurb on some editions of the novel.

The story is told in the witty, wisecracking voice of 22-year-old Rosemary Cooke. In 1996 Rosemary is a student at the University of California. Here she hopes to free herself from the painful associations of Bloomington, Indiana, where she was raised. After she is given her mother's journals from the 1970s, Rosemary's narrative casts back to 1979: the year her life changed forever. As a five-year-old, Rosemary is unexpectedly sent to stay with her grandparents and, when she returns home, finds that her sister, Fern, has gone. Fern's disappearance is shrouded in secrecy and, within this silence, each member of the Cooke family slowly falls apart. Rosemary's father takes to drinking, her mother has a breakdown and her beloved older brother, Lowell, withdraws into hostile introversion. Shortly afterwards, Lowell leaves home and disappears off the family's radar. All that the Cookes know of his whereabouts is that he is wanted by the FBI as an animal rights activist. As Rosemary tries to reconstruct the past from her adult perspective, her narrative circles around the precise events surrounding Fern's disappearance. Desperate to know the truth, she is also afraid of it, as she knows she will have to come to terms with her own role in events.

A key component of the plot is the role of Rosemary's father as a professor of animal psychology. The novel was inspired partially by real psychological experiments that took place on animals in the 1930s, and partially by conversations the author had with her father (also an animal behaviourist) about animal intelligence. In the course of the story, many difficult questions are raised concerning animal welfare and there is no denying that parts of the novel are distressing, particularly for animal lovers. Rosemary's narrative never becomes a diatribe, however, and while she observes the suffering that animals undergo during experimentation, she also acknowledges the advancements in medicine that this has led to: "Nobody's arguing these issues are easy." Fowler's point is that just because those questions aren't easily answerable doesn't mean we shouldn't ask them. For both the reader and Rosemary, the story requires the courage to face the truth.

On a wider level, Fowler's novel is a moving and intelligent exploration of what makes us human. Although its dark subject matter may be off-putting to some, readers should be assured that this novel is not a depressing read. While raising serious food-for-thought, Rosemary's narrative is always engaging, frequently humorous and captures real moments of joy, conveying both the pleasures and sufferings of being alive. Perfect for book groups in both the ethical questions it raises and its compelling narrative, *We Are All Completely Beside Ourselves* is sure to prompt interesting discussion.

ABOUT THE AUTHOR

Karen Joy Fowler is an American author who currently lives with her husband in Santa Cruz, California. Born in 1950 in Indiana to learned parents (her father was a professor and her mother a teacher), she went on to attend the University of California, Berkeley, and majored in political science. The year she graduated, she also married and then went on to take a masters at UC Davis. The next few years of Fowler's life were taken up by rearing her two young children. On her 30th birthday, however, she made the decision to become a writer. After taking a creative writing class, she began to make a name for herself writing short science fiction stories. Her debut novel, *Sarah Canary*, met with an enthusiastic response from critics but the author became a household name with the publication of the hugely popular *The Jane Austen Book Club* (2004), which was also made into a movie. Fowler's other novels include *Sister Noon*, *Wit's End* and *The Sweetheart Season*. *We Are All Completely Beside Ourselves* won the PEN/Faulkner award and was shortlisted for the Man Booker Prize.

IN A NUTSHELL

A witty and heart-breaking exploration of what makes us human, how we treat non-humans, and the fine line between the two

THEMES

Human and animal nature; animal welfare; family; love; sibling rivalry; loss; grief; forgiveness

DISCUSSION QUESTIONS

1/ The story is told entirely from the perspective of Rosemary. Did you enjoy Rosemary's narrative voice and, if so, what did you like about it? How does Rosemary's tone of voice contrast with the subject matter of her story? Would you have liked to hear the story from any of the other characters' points-of-view?

2/ The publicity surrounding this novel has meant that few readers begin it without already knowing the secret concerning Fern's identity. Why does Rosemary initially withhold this information from the reader? If you were already aware of the secret, did the spoiler impact on your enjoyment of the story?

3/ Why do Rosemary's parents adopt Fern in the first place? Do they share the same motivations for doing so? Are their reasons for sending Fern away understandable? What would you have done in their position?

4/ Did you find the author's portrayal of Fern convincing? How did you feel about her?

5/ What impact does it have on both Rosemary and Fern to be brought up together? In what ways are they similar and are there any crucial differences between them? How is Rosemary's sense of identity affected after Fern's disappearance?

6/ The loss of Fern leaves each member of the Cooke family 'completely beside themselves'. Discuss the different ways in which they respond to that grief. Does the title have any other implications?

7/ What is it that attracts Rosemary to Harlow? What impact does she have on Rosemary's life?

8/ As a child Rosemary revels in her linguistic abilities but, in later life, becomes wary of language. Discuss the crucial role that language (both the ability to use it and the reverse) plays in the novel.

9/ Rosemary's non-linear narrative centres around her struggle to remember why Fern disappeared from her life. Discuss the way memory is represented as elusive, misleading or unreliable in the novel. Do you think many of us create 'screen memories' around portions of our past that we find painful to think about?

10/ Rosemary is haunted by guilt at the part she played in Fern's fate when she was a jealous five-year-old. Should she feel guilty for her actions? Was she responsible for Fern being sent away, or do you think this would have happened anyway?

11/ Towards the end of the novel Rosemary's narrative takes on the tone of a madcap farce. How does the author create this change of pace, and did it work for you? What do you think is its purpose?

12/ Rosemary states that she would like to, "get all the way to forgiveness". In the end, how far does she forgive herself and her family?

13/ How did you feel about Fern's eventual fate? Would a more upbeat ending to the novel have been credible or even desirable?

14/ Rosemary's narrative highlights the different ways animals are experimented on (psychological research, drugs trials, crash studies, cosmetics testing etc.) and the suffering they experience as a result. She also, however, acknowledges that some of this research has led to the combating of certain diseases and better treatments for others. In what circumstances, if at all, is animal experimentation acceptable?

15/ Rosemary develops a habit of sleeping for long periods when she wants to avoid painful situations. How does this reaction reflect society's attitude to animal welfare? Has reading this novel made you think about issues that you would usually rather not dwell on?

FURTHER READING

The Jane Austen Book Club, Karen Joy Fowler
Water for Elephants, Sara Gruen
Barkskins, Annie Proulx
Flight Behavior, Barbara Kingsolver
Life of Pi, Yann Martel

COMPARE AND CONTRAST TO

The Art of Racing in the Rain for its exploration of the relationship between humans and animals or *The Shock of the Fall* for the depiction of sibling relationships and guilt

We Were Liars
by E. Lockhart

FIRST PUBLISHED

2014

LENGTH

240 pages

SETTING

Beechwood (a fictional island off the coast of Massachusetts)

ABOUT THE BOOK

Cadence Sinclair Eastman is the seventeen-year-old narrator of *We Were Liars*. An accident has left Cadence an amnesiac - a condition apparently caused by trauma to her brain. Suffering paralysing migraines, Cadence spends her days numbed by medication, rattling around a huge house in Vermont with only her mother for company. Desperate to recall the details of her accident, which her family remain mysteriously tight-lipped about, Cadence recounts what little she remembers about the events leading up to it. She tells the reader that, during the summer she turned 15, her parents split up and she and her mother took their regular holiday to Beechwood, a private island owned by her wealthy grandparents. Also present were Cadence's aunts, Carrie and Bess; her cousins, Johnny and Mirren; and Gat, Johnny's best friend. Collectively known as 'the Liars', the group of teenagers were inseparable and Cadence clearly recalls that she and Gat began a romance. She has no idea, however, how these events led to her being discovered washed up by the sea, half-naked, with a brain injury. Since then, the other Liars have failed to reply to any of her correspondence and her mother packed her off to Europe with her father, rather than allow Cadence to return to Beechwood. As Cadence's seventeenth summer looms, however, she insists that she wishes to return to the family island, determined to get to the bottom of what really happened to her.

The categorisation of *We Were Liars* as a book for young adults belies the sophistication of this short, compelling novel. While Cadence's story covers some familiar teenage subject matter (parental divorce, first love and struggles with identity), it is also a critique of patriarchal power and irresponsibly held privilege. Lockhart includes references to *King Lear* and *Wuthering Heights* in her text and the novel shares themes with both these literary classics. Cadence's narrative voice is also startlingly original. Her spiky narrative is peppered with one-liners but also pulls no punches when it comes to conveying her pain to the reader. Sometimes breaking down into fractured sentences, it brilliantly conveys the thought processes of a girl who has been damaged both physically and emotionally.

While amnesia is becoming a well-worn trope in thrillers, Cadence's memory loss is much more than a convenient plot device. Her inability to recall a crucial part of her past is a metaphor for the Sinclair family's habit of keeping up appearances through silences and repression. Eager to maintain their image as a rich, beautiful and successful family, the adults refuse to talk about anything that might damage their notion of who they are. 'We were liars', it turns out, is a statement just as applicable to the adults as the gang of teenagers. As an amnesiac, Cadence is an unreliable narrator with a restricted understanding of events. As she sifts through her frustratingly limited memories and tries to guess what is not being said by her family, readers will be just as eager to get to the truth as she is. The secret, when it is finally revealed, is clever and devastating and will have many readers returning to the beginning to reconsider what they have just read.

ABOUT THE AUTHOR

E. Lockhart is the penname of the American writer Emily Jenkins. She was born in New York City and grew up in Cambridge and Seattle. Her father is the playwright Len Jenkin. Emily read English at Vassar, a New York liberal arts college, before going on to complete a doctorate in nineteenth century English literature at Columbia University. She teaches a creative writing for children

MFA at Hamline University. While writing picture books for younger children under her own name, she has also written a number of YA novels as E. Lockhart. These include *The Disreputable History of Frankie Laundau-Banks*, *Fly on the Wall*, *Dramarama*, and the Ruby Oliver quartet. *We Were Liars* became Amazon's #1 YA novel of 2014 and won the Goodreads Choice Award.

IN A NUTSHELL

A compelling tale of adolescent amnesia with a devastating twist

THEMES

Family; sibling rivalry; love; privilege; racism; power; mortality; greed

DISCUSSION QUESTIONS

1/ Cadence sometimes displays the classic characteristics of a self-centred teenager. Did you find her character likable, annoying, or a mixture of the two?

2/ Cadence's life begins to go wrong when her father leaves. What impact does his departure have on her? Why do you think he felt he could no longer be a part of the Sinclair family?

3/ As an amnesiac, Cadence cannot help being an unreliable narrator, as she can't remember key facts about events. There are, however, also instances where she gives an account of events which could be perceived as deliberately untruthful. Discuss the passage where Cadence claims her father shot her and the incident where she describes herself melting over her grandmother's sewing machine. Why does she choose to recount these particular moments in her life in this way?

4/ Cadence's narrative is sometimes disjointed and fragmented. Discuss the unusual sentence structure in these sections. What do they reveal about Cadence and what impact do they have upon the reader?

5/ Cadence, Mirren and Johnny are light-heartedly referred to as 'the Liars' by the adults. In what way has their upbringing encouraged them to become liars? Could the title of the novel equally refer to the rest of the Sinclair family?

6/ How does the island setting of the novel contribute to the mood and plot?

7/ Gat compares himself to Heathcliff in *Wuthering Heights* and Cadence to Catherine Earnshaw. What are the similarities between Cadence and Gat's relationship and the romance between Emily Brontë's characters? What are the differences? Why does Harris consider Gat to be a threat?

8/ Discuss the way Gat's influence on Cadence begins to change her view of the world.

9/ Cadence narrates a number of fairy tales which all revolve around three sisters and a king. How do they relate to Harris's relationship with his daughters? Why do Penny, Carrie and Bess allow themselves to be manipulated by their father?

10/ Discuss the way the Sinclair family equate property ownership with power. How does this relate to Cadence's decision to give away her possessions? Do you think there is a happy medium between the two attitudes?

11/ Why do the Liars set fire to Clairmont? Is it a heroic act or an example of adolescent histrionics? Does their crime achieve anything?

12/ During summer seventeen on Beechwood Cadence sees the other Liars, even though they are dead. Is there any other evidence to suggest that their ghosts are really present, or do you think Cadence is hallucinating?

13/ Did the revelation that the Liars are dead take you by surprise? In retrospect, what clues does the author slip in for the observant reader?

14/ By the end of the novel, Cadence has learned the truth about her accident and also confronted painful truths about herself. What does she gain from this process?

15/ The novel describes a tragedy that befalls a privileged American family. In what way does wealth prove to be a poisoned chalice for Cadence, her mother, and her aunts?

FURTHER READING

We Have Always Lived in the Castle, Shirley Jackson
Florence and Giles, John Harding
A Thousand Acres, Jane Smiley
Before I Go to Sleep, S.J. Watson
Wuthering Heights, Emily Brontë

COMPARE AND CONTRAST TO

The Catcher in the Rye for its quirky narrative style and depiction of damaged adolescence, or *My Name is Lucy Barton* for its exploration of family silences and repression

The Woman in Black
by Susan Hill

FIRST PUBLISHED

1983

LENGTH

208 pages

SETTING

Deliberately unspecified but clearly a fictional English town at the end of the nineteenth or the beginning of the twentieth century

ABOUT THE BOOK

Susan Hill's atmospheric novel begins on Christmas Eve in an unspecified year during the early twentieth century. As the protagonist and narrator, Arthur Kipps, listens to members of his family telling ghost stories around the fire, the eerie tales prompt his own memories of an encounter with supernatural forces many years before. His story is told in flashbacks and goes something like this …

Newly-qualified as a solicitor, young Arthur visits a small English town to settle the estate of Alice Drablow. When he arrives in the town, he finds that the locals are openly hostile and their odd behaviour seems to be linked to a mysterious woman he glimpses, dressed in black. To make matters worse, Eel Marsh House, Alice Drablow's former home, is an isolated property surrounded by marshes and is frequently cut off by the tide. Locals refuse to go near the property and, in order to complete his duties, Arthur must spend long stretches of time alone there. As events take an increasingly sinister turn, Arthur begins to piece together the mysterious story surrounding Eel Marsh House and the woman who haunts it. What he discovers there changes the course of his life irrevocably. First published in 1983, Hill's homage to the nineteenth century ghost story has become a contemporary classic, reflected in the novel's adaptation into a long-running stage play and a 2012 movie, starring Daniel Radcliffe. The key to *The Woman in Black*'s enduring popularity is its subtlety. In an age of increasingly gory horror movies, Hill's restrained prose continues to demonstrate that less can most definitely be more when it comes to creating an atmosphere of suspense and terror.

ABOUT THE AUTHOR

Susan Hill is an English novelist. Born in 1942 in Scarborough, Yorkshire, she attended Scarborough Convent Grammar School and went on to read English at Kings College, London. During her distinguished writing career Hill has published over 50 books and been awarded the Whitbread, Somerset Maugham and John Llewellyn Rhys prizes as well as appearing on the Booker prize shortlist. She was also awarded a CBE in 2012 for her services to literature. Her works range from literary novels and ghost stories to children's books and detective novels. While *The Woman in Black* remains her most famous novel, other well-known works include *Mrs de Winter* (a sequel to Daphne du Maurier's *Rebecca*); *I'm the King of the Castle* and the successful series of crime novels featuring the detective Simon Serrailler. Hill is married to Shakespeare scholar Stanley Wells and has two adult daughters. She lives in North Norfolk.

IN A NUTSHELL

An atmospheric ghost story proving that less is more when it comes to creating literary suspense

THEMES

The supernatural; maternal love; revenge; innocence; loss

DISCUSSION QUESTIONS

1/ From the beginning of the story, the reader is aware that Arthur

Kipps will survive his experience at Eel Marsh House, as he tells the story from the perspective of old age. Does this spoil the suspense of the novel? Would a present tense narrative have been more effective?

2/ Why do you think Hill decided to have an elderly Arthur telling the story? Do you think Arthur has managed to move on from the experience? In what ways has it changed him?

3/ In what way does the geographical setting of Eel Marsh House contribute to the novel's atmosphere and plot?

4/ Why do you think Arthur Kipps decides to stay on alone at Eel Marsh House, despite the omens and misgivings he experiences?

5/ When Arthur first arrives in Crythin Gifford, the residents deliberately withhold their knowledge about the woman in black. Why do they do this? Could you understand their reticence, or do they have a moral responsibility to warn Arthur? Do you think he would have heeded any warnings if they had been forthcoming?

6/ What is Sam Daily's role in the novel?

7/ In what way does the historical setting contribute to the novel's atmosphere? Why do you think Hill avoids precisely pinpointing when or where it is set? Did you have your own ideas about the novel's geographical or historical location? Would the story work equally well in a modern setting?

8/ In *The Woman in Black*, Susan Hill pays tribute to the nineteenth century novel by recreating the prose style of that era. Did you enjoy the archaic use of language in the novel?

9/ Which conventional devices of the traditional ghost story does Susan Hill use in the novel? How does she avoid cliché when using these tried-and-tested tropes? Which parts most unnerved you and why?

10/ Jennet's malevolence from beyond the grave is explained when we learn that she effectively lost her child twice. Did you feel that this was a convincing motivation for her indiscriminate killing of children? Did you feel any sympathy for Jennet's plight before she died? Did it occur to you that Jennet's curse might fall upon Arthur's future offspring?

11/ Do you think Jennet's thirst for revenge is sated with the death of Arthur's wife and child, or will she continue to haunt future generations?

12/ In what way can *The Woman in Black* be read as a story about the loss of innocence?

13/ Do you think *The Woman in Black* deserves its reputation as a contemporary classic?

14/ Would you normally choose to read fiction with a focus on the supernatural? What is it about haunted house stories, in particular, that tap into our deepest fears?

15/ Much of the novel's power lies in elements which are left to the reader's imagination. Does this make film and theatre adaptations of the novel problematic? Have you seen a theatrical adaptation of *The Woman in Black* or the film version? If so, how were the most frightening moments of the story conveyed?

FURTHER READING

The Mist in the Mirror, Susan Hill
The Woman in White, Wilkie Collins
The Girl on the Landing, Paul Torday
All Things Cease to Appear, Elizabeth Brundage
Beyond Black, Hilary Mantel

COMPARE AND CONTRAST TO

The Loney for its conjuring of a sinister, atmospheric landscape

The Year of the Runaways
by Sunjeev Sahota

FIRST PUBLISHED

2015

LENGTH

484 pages

SETTING

Sheffield (England) and India

ABOUT THE BOOK

Set in the northern city of Sheffield in 2003, *The Year of the Runaways* recounts a year in the lives of four main characters: three young men from Pakistan and a British-Indian woman. Randeep has entered the UK on a marriage visa to British-born Narinder, Avtar has arrived on a student visa, and Tochi has entered the country illegally hidden in the back of a lorry. The three men share a house with nine other migrant workers, while Narinder lives alone in the flat Randeep has rented as their 'marital home'.

The first half of the novel alternates between chapters describing the characters' attempts to settle in their bleak new surroundings and sections explaining how they have come to be there. The first story is that of Tochi, who was a rickshaw driver in Pakistan. Tochi and his family are Chamaar: Indians viewed as untouchable by those of higher castes. During a period of zealous Hindu nationalism in the country, Tochi and his family become the victims of violent persecution. Randeep comes from a more privileged background but decides to leave the country to help his family when his father falls ill and also to escape from a shameful incident he would rather forget. Avtar, unable to find work in Pakistan, leaves out of economic desperation and hopes that success in the UK will mean he can marry Randeep's sister. Narinder, meanwhile, who is a devout Sikh, has married Randeep in a selfless attempt to offer someone less fortunate a better life. In doing so, however, she runs the risk of being disowned by her family.

Once the characters' backstories are established, the second half of the novel describes the grim realities of their new lives. The young men soon find that their dreams of becoming rich in the UK were, at best, naïve. With jobs hard to come by, they live in cramped squalor and tensions in the shared house mount as the men are forced to compete for low paid, menial jobs. Working as casual labour on building sites, in fast food restaurants and even down sewers, Avtar and Randeep struggle to feed themselves adequately after sending a proportion of their wages home. Additional pressure comes from the lurking presence of ruthless loan sharks and persistent immigration officials. Meanwhile, Tochi finds that he is still persecuted for his caste, even in the UK.

This novel's shortlisting for the Man Booker Prize reflects not only the currency of its subject matter but also the quality of Sahota's writing. In the context of the world immigrant crisis, this book is a necessary reminder of the humanity of those people who, for various reasons, choose to leave their homelands. Sahota provides a powerful insight into Indian culture, the reasons Indian migrants travel to the UK and, perhaps most importantly, the grinding hardship of many of their lives once they arrive. Anyone who believes that admission to the West offers easy lives to immigrants will think again after reading Sahota's novel. While the author undoubtedly intends his novel to be a damning portrait of prejudice and economic slavery, he never clubs the reader over the head with his message. One of the great qualities of this novel is its subtlety. By relating the day-to-day lives of his flawed yet sympathetic characters, Sahota immerses readers in the experiences of a hidden community and leaves us to ponder on their lives long after finishing the novel.

ABOUT THE AUTHOR

Sunjeev Sahota was born in 1981 in Britain. He spent his early childhood in the East Midlands town of Derby before moving to the northern town of Chesterfield with his family. Having never read a novel until he was eighteen years old, Sahota discovered the joys of fiction late in life and took a maths degree at Imperial College, London. Before becoming a full-time writer he worked for an insurance company and a building society. His debut novel, *Ours are the Streets*, was also set in Sheffield and offered an insight into the mind of a young Muslim extremist set on becoming a suicide bomber. The novel earned him a place on the 2013 Granta's Best of Young British Novelists list. Sahota lives with his wife and two children in Sheffield.

IN A NUTSHELL

A moving and powerful insight into the lives of Indian immigrants in the UK

THEMES

Exile; isolation; duty; sacrifice; prejudice; poverty; shame; honour; love

DISCUSSION QUESTIONS

1/ *The Year of the Runaways* revolves around four main characters: Avtar, Randeep, Narinder and Tochi. Which of them did you find the most sympathetic and why?

2/ In the first part of the novel, events in Sheffield are interwoven with flashbacks to the lives of Avtar, Randeep and Tochi in India. What do these flashbacks add to the narrative?

3/ Avtar, Randeep and Tochi all travel to England in search of a better life. Discuss what each of the men has to go through in order to reach the UK and how their lives pan out when they get there. How does the reality of England compare to the dream? Was there an aspect of their living conditions that particularly shocked you?

4/ In Sheffield, Avtar, Randeep and Tochi share a house with nine other men. Discuss the impact that insufficient money and competition over jobs has on the dynamics of the household. Do you think it would be possible to maintain a moral code in such an environment?

5/ Duty and sacrifice are major themes in the novel. Discuss the conflict the main characters feel between their personal desires and what they perceive to be their duty.

6/ Narinder keenly feels the responsibilities the privileged have towards the poor and suffering. Discuss the different ways in which she tries to help others. How do her religious beliefs and her concept of performing good works change as the novel progresses? Does she succeed in making a difference?

7/ Discuss the way Narinder's conflicts illustrate the issues faced by women in Indian society in general. Do you think she achieves either freedom or happiness by the end of the novel?

8/ Discuss the way Tochi's identity as a low-caste 'chamaar' shapes his life in India and in the UK. Did the scale of racial prejudice he encounters from other Indians surprise you? Does the novel critique any other aspects of Indian culture?

9/ Throughout the novel the author sprinkles the text with Punjabi words and phrases, such as the greeting, 'Sat sri akal' (God is the Ultimate Truth). Why do you think he chooses not to provide a glossary? Did the use of Indian dialect disrupt or enhance your reading experience?

10/ A notable proportion of the text is spent describing the characters preparing food. What significance does food and its preparation take on for the Indian characters in the book?

11/ The characters in the novel are capable of acts of cruelty and injustice but also random acts of kindness. Discuss the incidents that illustrate this duality of the human spirit. Would you say humanitarianism ultimately triumphs over barbarity in *The Year of the Runaways*?

12/ Discuss the different forms of loneliness experienced by the characters in the novel. Does the love story between Narinder and

Tochi arise purely out of mutual loneliness or something deeper?

13/ The epilogue of the novel is set over a decade later. Discuss the ways in which the main characters have changed and developed. Were you surprised at their fates?

14/ In the current worldwide immigration crisis, many people are sympathetic to those fleeing conflict in their homelands but are much less welcoming to economic migrants like Avtar, Randeep and Tochi. Did reading the novel prompt you to reassess your opinions about economic immigrants? Did you feel that the characters' reasons for emigrating were understandable?

15/ The literary critic, Ron Charles, has hailed *The Year of the Runaways* as "*The Grapes of Wrath* for the 21st century". If you have read John Steinbeck's classic novel, what parallels can you see? Do you think Sahota's novel has the makings of a modern classic?

FURTHER READING

Brick Lane, Monica Ali
The Lives of Others, Neel Mukherjee
The God of Small Things, Arundhati Roy
A Suitable Boy, Vikram Seth
A Fine Balance, Rohinton Mistry

COMPARE AND CONTRAST TO

Americanah and *The Sympathizer* for their depiction of the immigrant experience

Bibliography

<u>Books</u>

Adichie, Chimamanda Ngozi. *Americanah*, Fourth Estate, 2013
Angelou, Maya. *I Know Why the Caged Bird Sings*, Hachette Digital, 2010
Atkinson, Kate. *Life After Life*, Doubleday, 2013
Atwood, Margaret. *The Heart Goes Last*, Bloomsbury, 2015
Backman, Fredrik. *A Man Called Ove*, Hodder & Stoughton, 2014
Burton, Jessie. *The Miniaturist*, Picador, 2014
Cline, Emma. *The Girls*, Random House, 2016
Doerr, Anthony. *All the Light We Cannot See*, HarperCollins, 2014
Donoghue, Emma. *Room*, Picador, 2010
Ferrante, Elena. *My Brilliant Friend*, Europa Editions, 2011 (translation by Ann Goldstein)
Filer, Nathan. *The Shock of the Fall*, The Borough Press, 2014
Fitzgerald, F. Scott, *The Great Gatsby*, Penguin Modern Classics, 2005 reprint
Flynn, Gillian. *Gone Girl,* Orion Books, 2012
Fowler, Karen Joy. *We Are All Completely Beside Ourselves*, Penguin, 2013
Gale, Patrick. *A Place Called Winter*, Tinder Press, 2015
Green, John. *The Fault in our Stars,* Penguin, 2012
Haig, Matt. The Humans, Canongate, 2013
Hawkins, Paula. *The Girl on the Train*, Doubleday, 2015
Hill, Susan. *The Woman in Black*, Vintage, 1998 reprint edition
Hosseini, Khaled. *And the Mountains Echoed*, Penguin, 2013
Hurley, Andrew Michael. *The Loney*, John Murray, 2015
Ishiguro, Kazuo. *The Buried Giant*, Faber and Faber, 2015
Ivey, Eowyn. *The Snow Child*, Tinder Press, 2012
James, Henry. *The Turn of the Screw and Other Stories*, OUP, 2008 reprint edition
McInerney, Lisa. *The Glorious Heresies*, John Murray, 2015
Monk Kidd, Sue. *The Invention of Wings*, Tinder Press, 2014
Moriarty, Liane. *The Husband's Secret*, Penguin, 2013
Lockhart, E. *We Were Liars*, Delacorte Press, 2014
Ng, Celeste. *Everything I Never Told You*, Blackfriars, 2014

Nguyen, Viet Thanh. *The Sympathizer*, Grove/Atlantic, 2015
Obreht, Téa. *The Tiger's Wife*, Random House, 2011
Orwell, George. *1984*, Penguin Classics reprint, 2004
Sahota, Sunjeev. *The Year of the Runaways*, Picador, 2015
Salinger, J.D. *The Catcher in the Rye*, Penguin, 1960 reprint
Shaffer, Mary Ann & Barrows, Annie. *The Guernsey Literary and Potato Peel Pie Society*, Bloomsbury, 2010
St. John Mandel, Emily. *Station Eleven*, Pan Macmillan, 2014
Stedman, M.L. *The Light Between Oceans*, Random House, 2012
Stein, Garth. *The Art of Racing in the Rain*, HarperCollins, 2008
Stockett, Kathryn. *The Help*, Penguin, 2009
Strout, Elizabeth. *My Name is Lucy Barton*, Random House, 2016
Tartt, Donna. *The Goldfinch*, Little Brown, 2013
Waters, Sarah. *The Paying Guests*, Virago, 2014
Whitehead, Colson. *The Underground Railroad*, Doubleday, 2016
Zevin, Gabrielle. *The Collected Works of A.J. Fikry*, Little Brown, 2014

Websites

www.anthonydoerr.com
www.celesteng.com
www.colsonwhitehead.com
www.elenaferrante.com
www.elizabethstrout.com
www.emilylockhart.com
www.emmadonoghue.com
http://eowynivey.com/
www.galewarning.org
http://www.garthstein.com/
www.gillian-flynn.com
www.johngreenbooks.com
http://karenjoyfowler.com/
www.kateatkinson.co.uk
http://khaledhosseini.com/
http://www.lianemoriarty.com
www.matthaig.com
www.margaretatwood.ca
www.mayaangelou.com
www.paulahawkinsbooks.com

www.sarahwaters.com
http://suemonkkidd.com/
www.susanhill.org.uk
www.vietnguyen.info/home

Articles

Suad Khatab Ali. 'The Sympathizer.' *New York Journal of Books*, 7 April 2015

Alexandra Alter. 'Welcoming the dark twist in her career: Paula Hawkins's journey to The Girl on the Train.' *The New York Times*, 30 January 2015

Margaret Atwood. 'Are humans necessary? Margaret Atwood on our robotic future.' *The New York Times*, 4 December 2014

Hannah Beckerman. '*My Name is Lucy Barton* by Elizabeth Strout review - powerful storytelling.' *The Guardian*, 2 February 2016

Sarah Begley. 'The historical truth behind Elena Ferrante's Neapolitan novels.' *Time Magazine*, 31 August 2015

Gina Bellafonte. 'Holden Caulfield Redux. A Look at the New York Novel "The Goldfinch" by Donna Tartt.' *The New York Times,* 28 Nov 2013

Joanna Biggs. 'I was blind, she a falcon.' *The London Review of Books*, 10 September 2015

J.W. Bonner. 'Interview with Elizabeth Strout.' *KIRKUS*, 12 January 2016

Julie Bosman. 'Writer Brings in the World While She Keeps It At Bay Donna Tartt Talks, a Bit, About The Goldfinch.' *The New York Times,* 20th Oct 2013

Randy Boyagoda. '*The Sympathizer* by Viet Thanh Nguyen review - a bold artful debut.' *The Guardian*, 12 March 2016

Paul Burston. 'A Place Called Winter by Patrick Gale book review: A powerful tale of intolerance.' *The Independent*, 1 April 2015

Carmen Callil. 'All the Light We Cannot See by Anthony Doerr review - a story of morality, science and Nazi occupation.' *The Guardian*, 17 May 2014

Nora Caplan-Bricker. 'How Jane Austen Helped Inspire Elena Ferrante's Disappearing Act.' *Slate*, 20 October 2015

Philip Caputo. '*The Sympathizer* by Viet Thanh Nguyen.' *The New York Times*, 2 April 2015

Steph Cha. 'All the Light We Cannot See pinpoints two lives in war.' *LA Times*, 23 May 2014

Ron Charles. 'Oprah's Book Club Pick: *The Underground Railroad* by Colson Whitehead.' *The Washington Post*, 2 August 2016

Ron Charles. '*The Sympathizer*: A cerebral thriller about Vietnam and its aftermath.' *The Washington Post*, 31 March 2015

Ron Charles. 'Pulitzer-winner Viet Thanh Nguyen thanks minority writers who "blazed the path."' *The Washington Post*, 19 April 2016

Ron Charles. 'The Year of the Runaways review: The Grapes of Wrath for the 21st century.' *The Washington Post*, 21 March 2016

Alexander Chee. 'The Leftovers 'Everything I Never Told You,' by Celeste Ng.' *The New York Times*, 15 August 2014

Alex Clark. "On a quest with Kazuo Ishiguro." *The Guardian*, 21 February 2015

Laura Collins-Hughes. '*My Name is Lucy Barton* weaves a delicate balance.' 9 January 2016

Claire Coughlan. 'A Place Called Winter, by Patrick Gale: a novel that gets under your skin.' *The Irish Times*, 28 March 2015

Amanda Craig. 'Reviewed: *Life after Life* by Kate Atkinson.' *New Statesman*, 21 March 2013

Anthony Cummins. '*The Heart Goes Last* by Margaret Atwood, review: a curious hybrid.' *The Telegraph*, 30 September 2015

Rachel Cusk. 'The Paying Guests by Sarah Waters review - satire meets costume drama.' *The Guardian*, 15 Aug 2014

Lucy Daniel. 'The Paying Guests by Sarah Waters, review: eerie, virtuoso writing.' *The Telegraph*, 30 Aug 2014

Lucy Daniel. 'The Tiger's Wife by Tea Orbreht – review.' *The Telegraph*, 10 March 2011

Lucy Daniel. 'The Year of the Runaways by Sunjeev Sahota, review: of our time.' *The Telegraph*, 20 August 2015

Stevie Davies. 'Bright and dark: Stevie Davies is entranced by a bibliophilic jeu d'esprit.' *The Guardian*, 8 Aug 2008

Michelle Dean. 'Anthony Doerr: "I grew up where to call yourself a writer would be pretentious."' *The Guardian*, 22 April 2015

Michelle Dean. 'Colson Whitehead: "My agent said: Oprah. I said: Shut the front door."' *The Guardian*, 17 August 2016

Linh Dinh. 'Apocalypse Lies.' *The Guardian*, 2 November 2001

Michael Dirda. 'Michael Dirda reviews 'The Paying Guests' by

Sarah Waters.' *The Washington Post*, 10 September 2014

Katrina Dodson. 'The Face of Ferrante: Katrina Dodson Interviews Ann Goldstein.' *Guernica Magazine*

Andray Domise. 'Review: Colson Whitehead's *The Underground Railroad* is a powerful reimagining of American history.' *The Globe and Mail*, 12 August 2016

Rachel Donadio. 'Italy's Great, Mysterious Storyteller.' *The New York Review of Books*, 18 December 2014

Rachel Donadio. 'Writing has always been a great struggle for me: Q & A with Elena Ferrante.' *The New York Times*, 9 December 2014

Emily Dugan, 'The Year of the Runaways, by Sunjeev Sahota, book review: New country, old problems.' *The Independent*, 13 June 2015

Helen Dunmore. 'A Place Called Winter by Patrick Gale review – an elegy for the disappeared.' *The Guardian*, 10 April 2015

Claire Fallon. 'The Bottom Line: *The Heart Goes Last* by Margaret Atwood.' *Huffington Post*, 2 October 2015

Joan Frank. 'The Story of a New Name: review.' *The San Francisco Chronicle*, 13 December 2013

John Freeman. 'Talking to Pulitzer Prize-winning writer Viet Thanh Nguyen.' *Literary Hub*, 18 April 2016

Jessica Gelt. 'Viet Thanh Nguyen tackles Vietnam War's aftermath in *The Sympathizer*.' *Los Angeles Times*, 10 April 2015

David Gilbert. 'Donna Tartt.' *Vanity Fair*, Nov 2013

James Grainger. '*The Sympathizer* by Viet Thanh Nguyen: review.' *The Toronto Star*, 27 April 2015

Suzi Feay. 'The Girl on the Train by Paula Hawkins review - a skilful memory-loss thriller.' *The Guardian*, 8 January 2015

Molly Fischer. 'Not for Grown-ups: The Tiger's Wife by Tea Obreht.' *The Observer*, 3 September 2011

John Freeman. 'All the Light We Cannot See by Anthony Doer.' *The Boston Globe*, 3 May 2014

Sarah Hampson. 'Review: Elizabeth Strout's *My Name is Lucy Barton* is an exploration of memory.' *The Globe and Mail*, 22 January 2016

M. John Harrison. '*The Heart Goes Last* by Margaret Atwood review - rewardingly strange.' *The Guardian*, 23 September 2015

Tom Holland. 'The Buried Giant Review - Kazuo Ishiguro ventures into Tolkien territory.' *The Guardian*, 4 March 2015

Doug Johnstone. 'The Heart Goes Last, by Margaret Atwood - book review: Travels in Dystopia, with Doris Day and Marilyn.' The Independent, 27 September 2015

Sam Jordison. 'Not the Booker prize 2013: Life After Life by Kate Atkinson.' The Guardian, 27 August 2013

Michiko Kaktani. 'Review: 'Underground Railroad' Lays Bare Horrors of Slavery and its Toxic Legacy.' The New York Times, 2 August 2016

Michiko Kakutani. 'Review: The Year of the Runaways, About Fighting for Scraps in a New Country.' The New York Times 21 March 2016

Kapka Kassabova. 'The Tiger's Wife by Tea Orbreht – review.' The Guardian, 12 March 2011

Lily King. 'Elizabeth Strout's My Name is Lucy Barton review.' The Washington Post, 4 January 2016

Stephen King. "Flights of Fancy Donna Tartt's Goldfinch." The New York Times, 10 Oct 2013

Josh Lacey. 'We Were Liars by E. Lockhart review - cunning, clever and absolutely gripping.' The Guardian, 5 July 2014

Dylan Landis. 'The Girls by Emma Cline.' The New York Times, 31 May 2016

Grace Z. Li. 'The Heart Goes Last - unsettling but not unsatisfying.' The Harvard Crimson, 9 October 2015

Lisa Locascio. 'The Sympathizer by Viet Thanh Nguyen.' Bookforum, 26 May 2015

Corrina Lothar. 'Book review: My Name is Lucy Barton.' The Washington Times, 11 February 2016

Elizabeth Lowry. "The Paying Guests by Sarah Waters." The Wall Street Journal, 19 Sept 2014

Sarah Lyall. 'Review: Margaret Atwood's The Heart Goes Last Conjures a Kinky Dystopia.' New York Times, 29 September 2015

Tim Martin. 'The Buried Giant by Kazuo Ishiguro Review: affectless fantasia.' The Guardian, 6 March 2015

Janet Maslin. 'Another girl gone in a tale of betrayal.' The New York Times, 4 January 2015

Janet Maslin. 'Light found in darkness of wartime: 'All the Light We Cannot See' by Anthony Doerr.' The New York Times, 28 April 2014

Charlotte Mendelson. 'The Paying Guests by Sarah Waters.' The Financial Times, 22 Aug 2014

Theo Merz. 'Matt Haig: "People handle you differently when they know you're depressive."' *The Telegraph*, 5 March 2015

Stephanie Merritt. 'The Heart Goes Last by Margaret Atwood review - madcap life-swapping dystopia.' *The Guardian*, 7 September 2015

Claire Messud. 'Elizabeth Strout's *My Name is Lucy Barton*.' *The New York Times*, 4 January 2016

Laura Miller. 'Practicing art with liberty and joy.' *The Slate Book Review*, 10 August 2016

Julie Myerson. 'The Loney by Andrew Michael Hurley review – horror days by the sea.' *The Guardian*, 23 August 2015

Leon Neyfakh. 'Margaret Atwood: the literary world's technology mascot.' *New Republic*, 7 May 2013

Connie Ogle. 'Review: *My Name is Lucy Barton* by Elizabeth Strout.' *Miami Herald*, 8 January 2016

Meghan O'Rourke. 'Elena Ferrante: the global literary sensation nobody knows.' *The Guardian*, 31 October 2014

Deborah Orr. 'Elena Ferrante: 'Anonymity lets me concentrate exclusively on writing.' *The Guardian*, 19 February 2016

Lawrence Osborne. 'The Sympathizer by Viet Thanh Nguyen.' *Financial Times*, 12 February 2016

Mike Peed. 'A Place Called Winter, by Patrick Gale.' *The New York Times*, 1 April 2016

Heidi Pitlor. 'The Girl on the Train by Paula Hawkins.' *The Boston Globe*, 3 January 2015

Minna Proctor. 'A Woman Escaped.' *Bookforum*, February 2014

Harry Ritchie. 'The Humans by Matt Haig: review.' *The Guardian*, 15 May 2013

Meg Rosoff. 'Fantasy Island: We Were Liars by E. Lockhart' *The New York Times*, 9 May 2014

Leyla Sanai. 'Review: *The Humans* by Matt Haig.' *The Independent*, 18 May 2013

Liesl Schillinger. 'A mythic novel of the Balkan wars.' *The New York Times*, 11 March 2011

Jennifer Schuessler. 'Colson Whitehead on slavery, success and writing the novel that really scared him.' *The New York Times*, 2 August 2016

Kamila Shamshie. 'The Goldfinch by Donna Tartt.' *The Guardian*, 27 Oct 2013

Kamila Shamsie. 'The Year of the Runaways by Sunjeev Sahota

review – a brilliant political novel about migrant workers in Sheffield.' *The Guardian*, 19 June 2015

Lionel Shriver. 'The woman on the first floor: Lionel Shriver on "The Paying Guests" by Sarah Waters.' *New Statesman*, 3 September 2014

Wendy Smith. 'The Resistance: The Guernsey Literary and Potato Peel Society by Mary Ann Shaffer and Annie Barrows.' *The Washington Post*, 3 August 2008

Susanna Sonnenberg. 'My Brilliant Friend by Elena Ferrante.' *The San Francisco Chronicle*, 1 October 2012

Alexandria Symonds. 'Still life with bombs, drugs and PTSD: Donna Tartt paints a masterpiece in The Goldfinch.' *The Observer*, 29 Oct 2013

Catherine Taylor. '*Those Who Leave and Those Who Stay* by Elena Ferrante Review: High Stakes Literature.' *The Telegraph*, 9 September 2014

Laura Thompson. 'Review: The Guernsey and Potato Peel Pie Society by Mary Ann Shaffer. Laura Thompson enjoys the charm of a story set on a wartime Channel Island.' *The Telegraph*, 30 Aug 2008

Boyd Tonkin. 'Book Review: The Goldfinch By Donna Tartt.' *The Independent*, 18 Oct 2013

Amanda Vaill. 'All the Light We Cannot See by Anthony Doerr.' *The Washington Post*, 5 May 2014

Juan Gabriel Vasquez. 'In Colson Whitehead's latest, the Underground Railroad is more than a metaphor.' *The New York Times*, 5 August 2016

William T Vollmann. 'Darkness visible. 'All the Light We Cannot See' by Anthony Doerr.' *The New York Times*, 8 May 2014

Simon Willis. 'The grandmaster of Naples.' *Intelligent Life Magazine*, December 2013

James Wood. 'Women on the verge: the fiction of Elena Ferrante.' *The New Yorker*, 21 January 2013

ABOUT THE AUTHOR

Kathryn Cope graduated in English Literature from Manchester University and obtained her master's degree in contemporary fiction from the University of York. She is a reviewer and author of The Reading Room Book Group Guides. She lives in the Peak District with her husband and son.

www.amazon.com/author/kathryncope